1/06

34.60

Primary Sources of World Cultures™

SWEDEN

A PRIMARY SOURCE CULTURAL GUIDE

Jason Porterfield

The Rosen Publishing Group's
PowerPlus Books™
New York

Published in 2004 by The Rosen Publishing Group, Inc.
29 East 21st Street, New York, NY 10010

First Edition

Library of Congress Cataloging-in-Publication Data

Porterfield, Jason.
Sweden : a primary source cultural guide / by Jason Porterfield.—1st ed.
    p. cm. — (Primary sources of world cultures)
Summary: An overview of the history and culture of Sweden and its people including the geography, myths, arts, daily life, education, industry, and government, with illustrations from primary source documents.
Includes bibliographical references and index.
ISBN 0-8239-3841-7 (library binding)
1. Sweden—Juvenile literature. [1. Sweden.]
I. Title. II. Series.
DL609 .P67 2003
948.5—dc21

2002012102

Manufactured in the United States of America

Cover images: Kalmar Castle, in Kalmar, Sweden, and three young Swedish girls dressed as Easter Witches. In the background is a portion of the Rök runestone.

Photo credits: cover (background), p. 34 © Macduff Everton/The Image Works; cover (middle), p. 70 © The Image Works; cover (bottom), pp. 48, 52 (top) © Swedish Institute; pp. 3, 118, 120 © 2002 GeoAtlas; pp. 4 (top), 8, 13, 65, 76 (bottom) © Superstock; pp. 4 (middle), 33 © Masakatsu Yamazaki/The Image Works; pp. 4 (bottom), 40, 43, 46 (top) © Werner Forman/Art Resource; pp. 5 (top and bottom), 7, 9 (top), 15 (bottom), 18, 49, 53 (top), 60, 73 (top), 76 (top), 82 (top), 89 (top), 94, 99, 101, 117 (bottom) © SRT; pp. 5 (middle), 25 © Maps.com/Corbis; pp. 6, 67, 75 (bottom), 88 (bottom) © Macduff Everton/Corbis; pp. 9 (bottom), 10, 28 (top and bottom) © Viesti Associates Inc.; p. 11 © Ake Lindau/Okapia 1989/Photo Researchers, Inc.; pp. 12, 17, 19, 116 (middle) © Photri, Inc.; p. 14 © Stone/Getty Images; p. 15 (top) © Hubert Stadler/Corbis; pp. 20 (top and bottom), 21, 39, 53 (bottom), 90, 96 (top), 97, 109 (top), 119, 121 © Matton Images; pp. 22, 23, 75 (top), 78 (top), 82 (bottom), 83, 89 (bottom), 98 (bottom), 116 (top) © Hulton/Archive/Getty Images; p. 24 © Giraudon/Art Resource; pp. 26 (top), 29 (top), 30, 31, 32 (top), 35, 36, 44, 47, 63, 79, 85, 86, 88 (top), 91, 92 (top and bottom), 93, 104, 110 (top and bottom), 111 © IBL Picture Agency Sweden; pp. 26 (bottom), 27 (top), 42, 59, 62, 81 © The Granger Collection; p. 27 (bottom) © National Trust/Art Resource; p. 29 (bottom) © AFP/Corbis; pp. 32 (bottom), 50, 52 (bottom), 54 (top), 55, 56, 71 (top and bottom), 95, 98 (top), 100, 103, 107, 108 (bottom), 109 (bottom), 117 (top) © ScanPix; p. 37 © Uppsala University Collection/Bridgeman Art Library; pp. 41, 57 © Werner Forman Archive; p. 45 © Hans Strand/Corbis; pp. 46 (bottom), 58, 61 (top and bottom), 66 © Mary Evans Picture Library; pp. 51, 54 (bottom) 116 (bottom) © AP/Wide World Photos; pp. 64, 96 (bottom), 102 © Alex Farnsworth/The Image Works; p. 68 © Royalty-Free/Corbis; p. 69 © Aurora Photos; p. 72 © Reuters NewMedia Inc./Corbis; pp. 73 (bottom), 108 (top) © National Geographic; p. 74 (top) © Christie's Images/Superstock; p. 74 (bottom) © Marvin E. Newman/Woodfin Camp & Associates; p. 77 © Nik Wheeler/Corbis; pp. 78 (bottom), 80, 84 © Bettmann/Corbis; p. 105 © Chad Ehlers/International Stock; p. 106 © Steve Raymer/Corbis.

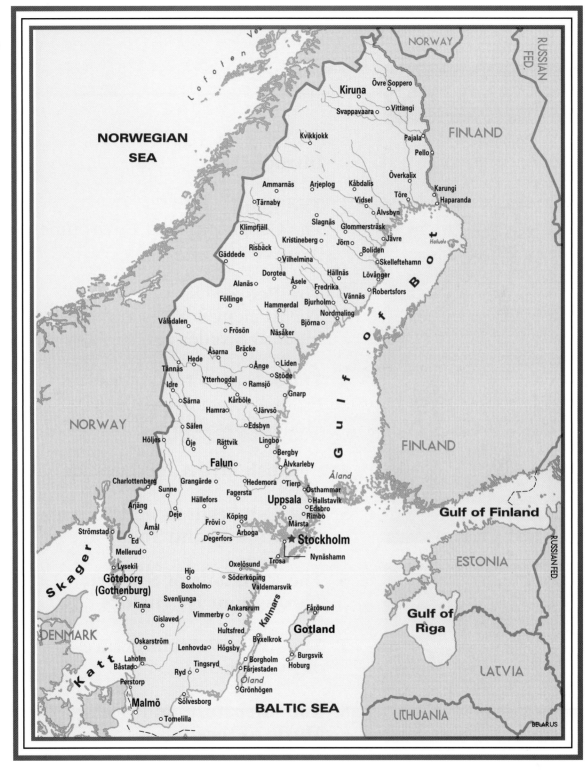

CONTENTS

INTRODUCTION

I n the north of Sweden, people herd reindeer for a living. To the south, they build mobile phones. This country, once home to the fiercest warriors in the world, has been neutral for almost two hundred years. Americans associate Sweden with the peppy music of ABBA and the dark visions of filmmaker Ingmar Bergman. Sweden dominated the world's attention for a week in 1986 when an unknown assassin shot and killed the humanitarian Prime Minister Olof Palme. A quiet, nonviolent people, Swedes love the outdoors and physical activity, although snow covers the ground for most of the year in some areas. Sweden is truly a land of contrasts.

Sweden's hardworking people enjoy some of the highest wages in the world and an excellent quality of life. The high taxes they pay fund a government system intended to keep the population safe, happy, and healthy from birth to death. They extend this concern for the human condition to impoverished people across the world, who in turn see so many blue and gold Swedish flags adorning aid packages that they may believe this small country to be a global power.

Children around the world recognize the name Pippi Longstocking. Each November, adults all take note of the brilliant Nobel laureates honored by Sweden,

This aerial photo of Stockholm *(left)* shows the city's busy harbor as well as Sweden's archipelago. The multitude of islands within the archipelago offer Swedes many opportunities for boating, fishing, and other outdoor activities. A small road cuts through Sweden's countryside *(above)* in the scenic region of Sydsverige, Sweden.

This is an aerial view of Lake Vättern near Hastholmen, Sweden. Lake Vättern, located in southern Sweden, is the country's second largest lake. At the center of the lake is Visingsö, the island of kings and legends, where the first royal castle was built during the twelfth century.

recognizing the year's progress in culture and science. Craftspeople in Dalarna once created traditional Swedish handicrafts in home studios. Today, furniture following simple Swedish designs is marketed internationally. Most people enjoy a smorgasbord meal, although the American version rarely includes as much herring as a genuine *smörgåsbord* in Sweden!

A century ago, nearly all Swedes occupied red, wooden farmhouses in the country and worked the land. Now, over 90 percent live in cities. Swedish industries produce Saab cars and Electrolux appliances. Hasselblad cameras have traveled to the moon with NASA astronauts. For the most part, Swedes enjoy their jobs and belong to labor unions that ensure job security and good working conditions. Nevertheless, they feel a connection to the rural life they left behind. They love outdoor activities, and take holidays in the country whenever possible.

Swedish Vikings once traveled the known world, establishing trade routes and colonies. Later, the Swedish Empire ruled the entire Baltic Region until losing its

conquests, shrinking down to Sweden's present-day boundaries. Sweden shares common cultural roots with the other Scandinavian countries, which sometimes leads to political alliances. In 1995, Sweden joined the European Union (EU), forging its firmest tie to mainland Europe in centuries. The new Öresund Link connects Sweden to Denmark, offering the best new economic bridge to mainland Europe since the Viking trade routes.

In July 2000, Sweden's King Gustav XVI and Denmark's Queen Margrethe II opened the Öresund Link (shown above), a bridge joining their countries. Spanning 4.8 miles across the Danish straits, the Öresund Link arcs through the water in a "C" shape and is composed of a tunnel, a bridge, and an artificial island. At right is a mustard and rapeseed field during springtime in Scania, Sweden.

THE LAND

The Geography and Environment of Sweden

Sweden is a land of geographic extremes. Rugged mountains loom over the sparsely inhabited northern half of the country, while much of the population works, farms, and vacations on the milder fertile plains and cities to the south. Most towns and cities sit on the seacoast or near one of the many rivers, canals, and lakes. The Swedes value the environmental well-being of their country. Many private and government organizations protect the land, water, and biodiversity of the country. Historically, people's livelihoods have depended on Sweden's land and natural resources.

With an area of about 173,731 square miles (482,586 square kilometers), Sweden is roughly the size of California. It is the largest nation in Scandinavia and the third largest in Europe, behind France and Spain. Located in the eastern portion of Scandinavia, it is bound by Finland to the north and east, and the Gulf of Bothnia and the Baltic Sea to the east. The Kattegat strait of the North Sea, the Strait of Skagerrak, and the Strait of Öresund lie to the south, and Norway is to the west. Sweden's long peninsular coastline extends for over 4,400 miles

(7,000 kilometers). Thousands of islands dot the Swedish shores. Gotland, the largest island in the Baltic Sea, lies to the east of mainland Sweden, as does the island of Öland. About 15 percent of Sweden falls within the Arctic Circle.

During the summer months, wildflowers *(left)* are a lovely sight throughout much of the southern Swedish countryside. Sandstone rocks *(above)* are located on the west coast of Farö, Sweden.

There are forty-three kinds of tree species in Sweden. The north of Sweden is rich in birch trees, as seen in this photograph. These forests remain relatively untouched by humans and are affected only by reindeer grazing.

Sweden consists of three geographical regions: Norrland, Svealand, and Götaland. Each region has its own distinct natural character. Norrland, the largest area, constitutes the northern half of the country. Forests and mountains dominate Norrland. Much of the region reaches into the Arctic Circle, making it less hospitable to farmers, settlers, and tourists than the southern half of Sweden. Fewer people live here than in the other regions. With a total population of barely one million, only a few towns have more than fifty thousand people. One of these, Kiruna, is the site of one of the world's richest iron ore deposits. Other valuable minerals mined in this region include uranium, zinc, gold, silver, lead, and copper. The Sami, a native tribe distinct from other Swedes, make their home in much of the otherwise empty territory. There, they care for large herds of semi-domesticated reindeer, to which they owe their living.

Svealand, the physical and cultural heart of Sweden, contains a quarter of the country's geographical area. Three and a half million people live in this temperate region, most in large cities. Stockholm, Sweden's capital and largest city, extends across the island archipelago of Lake Mälaren. To the west, picturesque Värmland and Dalarna provinces hang on to the rural traditions of pre-industrial Sweden. Sweden's timber industry relies on Svealand's heavy forests.

Götaland is Sweden's heavily populated southern quarter. Two of the nation's largest cities, Göteborg and Malmö, lie on the region's southwestern coast. Götaland itself is divided into two regions: the plains of Skåne and the rocky Småland Highlands. Only about 7 percent of Sweden is farmland, most of it located in Skåne. The plains of Skåne are known as the "breadbasket of Sweden." Småland saw a mass emigration, mostly to the United States, in the nineteenth century, and its population remains low to this day.

Approximately one million people live in Stockholm, Sweden's capital. Referred to as the Venice of Northern Europe, Stockholm sits on several islands in Lake Mälaren. The Stockholm Globe Arena, the world's largest spherical building, holds a variety of events, such as hockey games and concerts. On June 17, 1992, it broke an audience record when 16,337 people attended a Bruce Springsteen concert.

Geographical Features

Sweden's rich landscape includes mountains, lakes, rivers, plains, forests, and islands, often within the same territory. Mountains on the northern borders give way to highlands, eventually descending to the southern lowland plains. Historically, the Swedes have relied on natural resources such as mining, timber, and waterways because of the

The mountains in Sweden near the Norwegian border tend to be round in shape with flat tops, resulting from a million years of erosion. This photograph shows Kebnekaise, the highest mountain in Sweden. At its foot are snow huts inhabited by the Sami people who live in this region.

scant amount of fertile farmland. Today, they work toward ecological preservation and consider the environmental consequences of using these natural resources.

Neither as big nor as imposing as some of mainland Europe's chains, Sweden's mountain peaks are nevertheless breathtaking in their natural splendor. Many of the most impressive are located in Norrland. The two tallest peaks, Kebnekaise (6,926 feet, 2,111 meters) and Sarektjåkko (6,854 feet, 2,089 meters), tower above the Kjølen mountain range bordering Norway. This chain dominates Norrland, contributing to the region's harsh natural extremes. The Småland Highlands, located in the western end of Götaland, more closely resemble hills than peaks. Few elevations rise above 500 feet (152.4 meters), giving the landscape a gently rolling quality.

Sweden contains about ninety thousand lakes, nearly a tenth of the surface area. Although Norrland boasts the most lakes, the three largest—Vänern, Vättern, and Mälaren—are all located in Svealand. Lake Vänern is the biggest lake in Scandinavia, and the fourth largest in Europe. It empties into the North Sea by way of the Göta River. Vänern's banks offer a prime site for industry, especially paper mills. When pollution started decimating its salmon population, environmentalists

This is River Valley in Sarek National Park. Four large rivers as well as many smaller streams criss-cross the national park. During times of high water, it is impossible to wade across even the smallest stream in this part of Sweden.

clamored for a cleanup. Today, Vänern's salmon are brought in from hatcheries. Vättern is the second largest lake, draining into the Baltic Sea by way of the Motala River. Stockholm perches between the eastern banks of the Baltic Sea and Lake Mälaren, within easy traveling distance of the hundreds of tiny islands scattered along its shores. These make popular holiday destinations.

Thousands of miles of rivers once played an important part in Sweden's economy, when trade and transportation relied largely on water. Most Swedish rivers spring from the western mountains and meander across the flatter lands to the east and south before finding their way to the ocean. Settlements once thrived within the extensive networks of waterways, and many present-day cities and towns rest along their banks.

Swedes added to the river networks by building canals and therefore linking important trade routes. The most notable

The Porjus Power Station, built in 1915, was one of Sweden's first hydroelectric power plants. Sweden is considered a world leader in renewable energy because it uses hydropower, wind, and biomass to generate electricity.

example is the Göta Canal, which runs east to west and utilizes lakes and rivers along its path. Lakes Mälaren, Vänern, and Vättern all act as links in this water route. Today, the Swedish people continue to profit by their natural waterways. The northern rivers, or *älvar*, of Norrland rush from the mountains with great force, providing hydroelectric plants with enough energy to supply about 15 percent of Sweden's electricity. The slightly calmer rivers to the south provide excellent habitats for fish hatcheries. In particular, the Ätran, Viskan, Lagan, and Nissan rivers host productive salmon hatcheries.

Sweden's sweeping coastline presents nearly every sort of beachfront imaginable. To the east and west, the coastal terrain is rocky and dotted with tiny little islands rounded by prehistoric glacier movements. This sort of coast, called *skärgård*, can be found around Stockholm and Göteborg. Other parts of the coastline are sandy, and Gotland Island's coast is made up of limestone rocks. Tourists and vacationers crowd the beaches during holiday seasons, despite the chilly water temperature. Coastal cities grew around Sweden's many harbors, the most important being Stockholm, Malmö, and Göteborg.

Infrastructure

Swedes travel with ease, thanks to excellent roads and a well-organized public transportation network. Smooth highways cross from one end of the country to the other. Railways are commonly used for shipping goods across Sweden. Most trains are electric and more environmentally friendly than trucks.

Swedes often take advantage of public transportation in both cities and outlying regions. Trains are a popular means of travel, particularly for tourists and commuters. Sweden's cities possess networks of trams, trains, and buses, providing convenient alternatives to driving short distances for errands or work. Ferries connect Swedish regions and provide routes to other Baltic countries.

The Öresund Link, completed in 2000, crosses the 10-mile (16-kilometer) strait between Sweden and Denmark. It consists of two parts. A 4.8-mile (7.8-kilometer) bridge—the longest in Europe—extends from Mälmo to a man-made island, where it drops into a long tunnel terminating in Copenhagen. Trains and automobiles carry passengers and freight between the two nations. The Swedes have high hopes for economic and cultural exchange using this new connection to the rest of Europe.

Göta Canal

One of Sweden's major engineering projects of the nineteenth century, the Göta Canal, spans 382 miles (614 kilometers). It cuts across Sweden from the mouth of Lake Mälaren southwest to Göteborg, where it empties into the Kattegat Strait. Begun in 1812 as an alternate route between the Baltic and North Seas, its original purpose was for Swedes to avoid paying outrageous shipping  tolls charged by Norway for the privilege of using the Öresund Strait. Massive channels were constructed, linking together a network of existing rivers and lakes. When the Göta Canal opened in 1832, it stood out as an engineering wonder. Few manmade waterways could challenge its size, and none could rival its beauty. Alas, the canal never achieved its full commercial potential. Soon after completion, Norway dropped its shipping tolls, and railways made the waterway obsolete. Today, Swedes still take pride in the Göta Canal, calling it "the Blue Ribbon." Thousands of tourists, including native-born Swedes, travel the length of the canal every year, enjoying the splendor of Sweden's folkloric landscape from one of the nation's most remarkable accomplishments.

Sweden's climate varies by region. However, the coldest month is February, and in northern Sweden the temperature can drop to as low as 40 degrees below zero Celsius (-40 degrees F). This glacier in Norrland, Sweden, was photographed during the winter season.

Climate

Sweden has a continental climate, with mild summer temperatures and cold winters. Precipitation falls mainly in the form of rain and snow. Svealand and Götaland receive between 22 and 23 inches of rain a year, while Norrland gets from 12 to 15 inches annually. Sweden is warmer than its northern location would suggest, although winters can be harsh. While Skåne's coldest weather lasts for less than two months, snow may cover the ground for eight months in the northern regions.

As with the winters, lengths of the growing seasons vary from the north to the south. Warm weather and ample sunlight allow farmers in Skåne about eight months to raise their crops. In the north, the days are shorter for much of the year, leaving farmers a scant four-month growing season. Luckily, northern lands are blessed by "the Midnight Sun." From May until the middle of July, the sun shines for twenty-four hours a day over much of Norrland. The longer days help the crops mature in time for harvest.

Plants and Animals

Sweden contains four distinct vegetative classes, each adapted to its own range. Mosses, lichens, and dwarf birches grow in the Alpine regions of the southwestern mountains and northern tundra. This biome occurs at altitudes over 1,600 feet (1,760 meters) in the north and 3,000 feet (3,300 meters) in the southwest. Birch woods begin where Alpine growth ends. Rowans, bird cherries, willows, and aspens thrive in these areas. Lichens and herbs form thick undergrowth along the woodland floor. The third region covers 57 percent of Sweden, mostly the lower northern territory and the Småland Highlands. These forests are mainly coniferous, consisting of Scotch pines and spruces. The northern section of the third region also includes lowland birches, rowans, and aspens, and the southern area contains an even greater mix of deciduous trees such as oaks, ashes, lindens, maples, and elms. Beech forests make up the fourth vegetation region, ancient groves found mostly in Skåne.

During the summer, the area above the Arctic Circle is known as the Land of the Midnight Sun. Winter months in the same area are called "Polar Night," due to the darkness of the days brought on by the lack of sun.

A lynx is a large cat with a short tail, but its pyramid-shaped ears with small tufts on the tips distinguish it from other large cats. Lynxes prey on roe deer and hare throughout Sweden. Elusive creatures, they are not typically seen by people.

These vegetation regions provide habitat for a diverse wildlife population. In the northern coniferous forests and birch woods, seldom seen wolves, bears, and lynxes still roam free, protected by law from hunters. Moose, badgers, otters, and elk, are common in all parts of Sweden. Tiny roe deer range throughout the south, while the Sami, an indigenous minority group, watch over vast herds of reindeer on the rugged northern tundra. Bird watching is popular in Sweden, and tourists and residents alike flock to its bird sanctuaries. Gulls, terns, and eider ducks live in great numbers along the coastline, while further inland one can find various songbirds, game birds, and birds of prey.

Sweden's lakes and rivers teem with trout, salmon, char, pike, and perch. Swedes find crayfish along the inland waterways, and consider them a delicacy. Fishing is still a major industry

In Sweden, the wolf population only numbers about one hundred. Wolves are now protected and efforts are being made to preserve these predators. Many groups of wolves are regularly heard in Värmlamd along the Norwegian border.

The once plentiful population of brown bears, which inhabit areas of northern Sweden, has dwindled to approximately 1,000. These animals are predators, but they are also known to eat ants and berries. During the winter months, brown bears hibernate for about six months, usually in a lair dug out in an anthill.

in Sweden, and worries about the dangers of overfishing are increasing. To offset this, hatcheries along the coast raise shrimp, herring, flatfish, mackerel, cod, and sprat.

A general love of nature, combined with concerns about environmental threats, inspired the establishment of twenty-six national parks in Sweden. The two largest, the Peljekajse and Abisko National Parks of Norrland, were Sweden's first national parks, and among the first in Europe. Today, most of the 3,990 square miles (6,423 square kilometers) of national parks are open to the public, except for a few restricted nature preserves. Visitors come to hike or climb, or merely to escape from their urban lives to delight in Sweden's natural beauty.

THE PEOPLE

2

The Ancient Swedes and the Modern Swedes

Most people stereotype the Swedes as tall, blond, and fair skinned. While this image endured for centuries and will most likely continue to do so, the face of Sweden has recently begun to change. The nation's people freely welcome refugees from other countries and cultures, who have begun adding to Sweden's diversity even as they blend into Swedish culture.

Early Sweden

Nomadic hunters first explored Sweden around 10,000 BC, following game north as the glacial ice receded. Farmers and herders began settling in the southern region by 3000 BC. The first distinct culture emerged about 1500 BC, named the Boat-Axe People for the shape of their stone axes. Trading amber and furs with other European tribes, they brought great wealth into Sweden before a climatic downturn and wars forced them to abandon their routes. They disappeared around 500 BC. The nomadic ancestors of modern Sweden, the fierce Svear, settled in the present-day Svealand region. By AD 750 they controlled everything in Sweden and had settled into a farming lifestyle.

The portrait of King Gustav I of Sweden *(left)* is dated approximately 1550. King Gustav I strengthened Sweden's trade, manufacturing and financial independence, as well as increased its military forces. Above is a prehistoric cave painting from the Bronze Age, which was created by the Boat-Axe People. This specific cave painting, found in Tanum, Bohuslan, Sweden, depicts three figures on a boat deck.

Dating from the ninth century, this stone carving was discovered in Gotland Island, Sweden. It shows Viking navigation rituals. From about AD 800 to AD 1100, Vikings were seafaring explorers who invaded the coastline of Europe and Russia. This stone carving is now housed in the Statens Historiska Museet in Stockholm, Sweden.

With peace came a growth in population, and the scant, rocky cropland could not produce enough food for the increased number of people. Circumstances forced many young men to turn toward the sea to make their fortunes. They became the Vikings: fierce warriors, shrewd traders, and fearless explorers. Sailing in speedy ships and heavily armed, they struck coastal villages and monasteries. After loading their ships with loot and captives—called thralls—they sailed from port to port, selling what they could and keeping the rest. While at home, the Vikings settled back into their lives as farmers and free landowners. Their thralls did much of the heavy work, earning their keep and occasionally their freedom. Viking society was governed by *things*, local representative bodies in which every free man had a voice. Though huge portions of the population were not represented, the *thing* later served as a model for representational democracies.

East by Sea

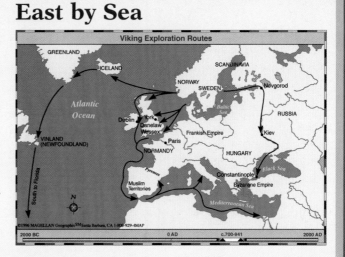

Viking Exploration Routes

While the Danish and Norwegian Vikings headed south and west, the Swedes ventured east, traveling through the Baltic Sea. When they reached a passable river, they took their ships as far inland as possible. The Swedes explored via waterways the places Europeans had forgotten during centuries of plague and war. They made contact with Baghdad, traded in Constantinople, and established colonies. Interested in protecting their trade routes, they founded Novgorod, conquered a place named Kiev, and kept the peace among the Slavic tribes living in the region. These tribes called their new rulers the Rus. Over time the colonizing Swedes became assimilated into the tribes and the term Rus came to mean all people in the area. The land itself is now known as Russia.

A Monarch's Land

Representative government fell out of favor when the first strong monarchical dynasty, the Folkungs, emerged in 1250. Enduring until 1374, the Folkung monarchs ended the thrall system and created the Riksdag, a kingdom-wide legislative body made up of representatives from four social classes—peasants, nobles, clergy, and a burgher class consisting of merchants and landowners. Sweden also became involved

in the Hanseatic League—an international trading system based in Germany—during Folkung rule. The Hanseatic League brought wealth into Sweden's ports and countryside, while Swedish culture took on many German characteristics.

In 1347 the Swedish nobility, feeling threatened by the increasing German influence and the growing wealth of the other classes, decided to end the Hanseatic League by setting up a Scandinavian trade monopoly. They established the Union of Kalmer, uniting Norway, Denmark, and Finland under Sweden's Queen Margaretha. The union ended in the 1460s, with the revolt of the miners, merchants, and peasants who wanted to continue trading with the Hanseatic League.

Denmark and Norway did not want to dissolve the union. They fought several wars with Sweden, resulting in a Danish victory during the early sixteenth century. Sweden's greatest hero, King Gustav Vasa, emerged to save Sweden, driving

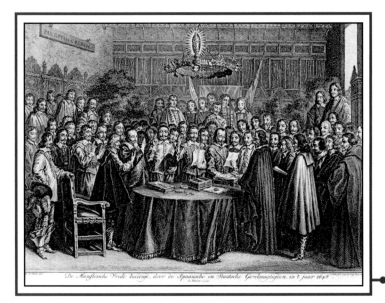

This Dutch line engraving from the seventeenth century depicts the Peace at Münster in May 1648, which took place after the Thirty Years' War between 1618 and 1648.

The Russian fleet defeating the Swedish fleet at Cape Hango in the Baltic Sea on July 26, 1714, is depicted in this eighteenth century line engraving. At this battle, Russia successfully invaded Sweden and began raiding Sweden's coastline in 1719.

out the Danes and declaring Swedish independence in 1523. He established a strong central government and encouraged trade, bringing about an age of peace and prosperity. Military victories by his descendents made Sweden one of the most powerful nations in Europe. By the end of the Thirty Years' War in 1648, Sweden controlled the entire Baltic region.

A series of wars and weak rulers resulted in the loss of most of Sweden's land, once again shattering the economy. Dissatisfaction with the royalty grew until the Riksdag finally wrested control of the country from the monarch in 1720. During this Era of Liberty, as it was known, the Riksdag appointed a chancellor and adopted a constitution. Despite these reforms, the two ruling parties, the "Caps" and the "Hats," spent more time squabbling than governing. When King Gustav III seized power from the Riksdag in 1772, all of Sweden breathed a sigh of relief. He enjoyed both absolute power and enormous popularity, establishing schools, hospitals, religious freedom, and sponsorship of the arts. The nobles, fearing his power, had him assassinated in 1792.

Displayed at the Blickling Property in Norfolk, Great Britain, this portrait of Peter the Great, tsar of Russia, depicts his defeat over Sweden at Poltava. As tsar, Peter the Great ruled Russia from 1682 until 1725 and fought a twenty-one-year war with Sweden for access to the Baltic Sea.

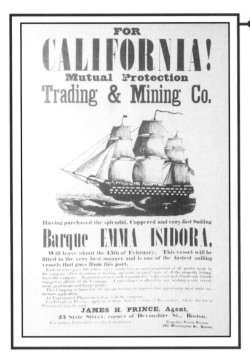

An original poster housed in the Swedish Emigrant Institute in Växjö, Sweden, encourages Swedes to work as miners by moving to California aboard the ship *Emma Isidora*.

Soon after, Sweden entered the Napoleonic Wars on the side of the French. They lost Finland to Russia in 1809, parting with a territory they had controlled for over six hundred years. Afterward, the people revolted and deposed King Gustav IV Adolf. A new constitution was written, dividing power between the monarch and the Riksdag. Their new king, a French field marshal who ruled under the name of Karl Johan, invaded Norway in 1814, Sweden's last militaristic action before entering a period of international neutrality.

Industrialization and the Modern Age

Before the 1800s, virtually all Swedes lived in the countryside as poor farmers. The Industrial Revolution gave them a chance to change their lives, and many flocked to the cities to work in factories. By the turn of the century a quarter of the population lived in urban areas. The countryside continued to empty, but for other reasons. The decades of neutrality once again brought a tremendous population boom. People seeking a way out of Sweden's oppressive poverty and with nowhere else to turn started

Housed at the Swedish Emigrant Institute in Växjö, Sweden, this historical photograph shows a crowd of people around the boat *Excelsior*, which traveled from Sweden to America carrying Swedish immigrants.

The cartoon titled "The Kindly Helping Hand," drawn by Arthur Sjögren in 1901, appeared in *Karbasesn* and depicts a demonstration for suffrage for all men in Sweden. In 1909, this movement achieved success.

leaving their crowded country behind. By 1900 almost a million people had emigrated from Sweden.

Sweden gradually grew more democratic during the nineteenth century. Constitutional changes made between 1864 and 1866 dissolved the estate system, making the Riksdag a bicameral elective body open to the 10 percent of Swedes who could vote and ending the monarch's personal power. People living and working in urban areas began forming labor unions during the 1880s, organizing in an effort to win suffrage. The labor unions led to the formation of the Social Democratic Party in 1889, giving the people a political voice within the Riksdag. Marches and demonstrations by the unions became widespread as Swedes sought a more democratic society. The people, through their work with unions and other organizations, gained universal suffrage. All men over twenty-four began to vote in 1909. Women won the right to vote in 1921.

Modern Sweden

Sweden entered the twentieth century with hopes of once again becoming a prosperous world power. The country sidestepped involvement in the bloodshed of World War I, but could not avoid the economic disaster that followed. The Great Depression struck Sweden hard in 1928, forcing the government to establish a welfare

World War II hero Raoul Wallenberg, shown here, is credited with saving the lives of 60,000 to 100,000 Jews. In 1945, Wallenberg disappeared after he was summoned by the Soviet military. Recent documents show that Stalin's secret police executed Wallenberg in 1947.

This photograph was taken during the opening of Sweden's parliament in 1939. During this session, Sweden's parliament began their policy of neutrality, which continues today.

state—government programs intended to redistribute the nation's wealth and help those in need. Sweden once again declared neutrality during the Second World War, but the policy was much harder to maintain. Some European nations, Norway and Finland in particular, criticized Sweden for allowing Nazi forces free passage through its countryside. Despite the position of the government, courageous Swedes like Raoul Wallenberg brought thousands of Jewish people and other homeless refugees into the country, saving them from horrible fates.

Sweden's wartime neutrality allowed it to keep most of its industry intact, and industrial production resumed as soon as hostilities ended in 1945. While other countries struggled to rebuild, Sweden transformed itself from one of Europe's poorer nations to its richest overnight. The ruling Social Democratic Party greatly expanded the scope of the welfare program, ensuring that the Swedish government could care for all its citizens from cradle to grave. High-quality nationalized health care helped give Swedes longer life expectancies than people of most other nations

These two Swedish girls are great examples of the blond hair and fair skin of their Swedish ancestors.

in the world. Public education, job security, and cultural institutions contributed to a high quality of life.

Today's Svensk

More than 85 percent of Sweden's population is descended from Nordic ancestors. As one might expect, they are usually tall and blond, with blue eyes and fair skin. Most live quiet, peaceful lives in towns or cities and are content to fit in with their neighbors and peers. A strong sense of fairness often governs their dealings with others, making them hesitant to interrupt during a conversation or keep someone waiting.

The typical Swede abhors loudness and rudeness, though most take care not to show their discomfort for fear of being rude themselves. They also dislike wasting time, and will be abrupt if they can complete a transaction with one word rather than four. Visitors to Sweden sometimes see their terseness as rude, but to the Swedes it is far worse to waste another person's time with meaningless conversation. Their politeness may seem uptight, but they are extremely friendly and helpful beneath their unassuming reticence.

Almost nine million people live in Sweden, a figure that has changed little over the past three decades. For many years, Sweden's birth rate and death rate nearly matched. Sweden's nearly microscopic population growth comes mainly from a recent wave of new immigrants entering the country since the end of World War II. Today, approximately one-fifth of Sweden's population has at least one foreign-born parent. People from other Nordic countries can become citizens after living in Sweden for two years. Immigrants from other parts of the world may choose to become Swedes after five years. Foreign nationals living in Sweden have many of the same rights and privileges as everyone else in the country, even before they become citizens.

Sweden's open immigration laws are enabling diversity to increase throughout the country. In order to help both native Swedes and new immigrants to adjust, many organizations have been established to ease cultural tensions.

Recent immigrants now face problems never experienced by their predecessors. During the economic downturn of the 1990s, unemployment among this group rose from 5 percent to over 20 percent. Some Swedes, anxious about their own economic situations, felt threatened by the newcomers. In June 1998, the government established the National Integration Board to help end the perception that immigrants were a group separate from other Swedes. This agency works toward fighting racism and discrimination while promoting equal rights for all.

Sweden is home to a few indigenous minority groups, among them Roma (Gypsies) and 300,000 native Finns. A small Roma population settled in Sweden nearly four hundred years ago, and more came during the nineteenth century. Most of the Finnish-speaking minority lives near the border with Finland, in communities left over from the time when Finland was considered part of Sweden.

The most visible and recognized minority group in Sweden are the Sami, nomadic reindeer herders who

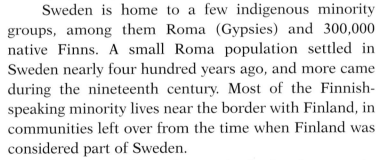

Since the sixteenth century, there has been a Romany, or gypsy, presence in Sweden. Currently about 25,000 Roma people live in Sweden, and laws established in December 1999 declared Roma a national minority, which prevents organizations from discriminating against them.

Sami, the original inhabitants of the Fennoscandian region, now settle lands north of the Arctic Circle and make their living by hunting and fishing. This young girl, wearing traditional dress, stands in the habitat of the Sami people.

occupy the mountainous regions of Norrland. For centuries they were referred to as Lapps, but now consider the term derogatory. Today, the English-speaking world uses the term Sami, a variation on Sabme, their name for themselves. Estimates put their total population, spanning across the border into Norway and Finland, between eighty thousand and 100,000 people. Though some of their traditions remain unchanged from centuries ago, the modern world is slowly encroaching upon the Samish way of life. Herders now use snowmobiles and mobile phones when tracking their reindeer, and most accept Christianity and speak Swedish. They are considered Swedish citizens and receive the same benefits as all others, but look after their own administrative affairs. Recent threats to their territory by miners and loggers mobilized many Sami to petition the government for the protection of their land and traditions. The Swedish government recognizes the validity of their claim, but environmentalists have raised concerns about the ecological impact of huge herds of grazing reindeer on the land of other wildlife. The herds contribute to soil erosion near rivers and streams. They can also strip an area of edible plants, leaving little for other creatures.

THE SWEDISH LANGUAGE

3

From Ancient Swedish to Modern Swedish

Välkommen till Sverige! You might hear this singsong Swedish welcome if you step off a plane in Stockholm. The Swedes call their country Sverige, derived from Svea rike, "land of the Sveas." An overwhelming majority of citizens, over 90 percent, consider Swedish their primary language.

Swedish—or svenska—is a Germanic language, belonging to the same family as Dutch, German, English, and the other Nordic languages. Many English words are similar or identical: for instance, the English word "call" is kalla in Swedish, "dog" (hound) is hund, "name" is namn, and so on. People with a knowledge of German learn Swedish very quickly, and can often grasp basic written Swedish without any background in the language.

The Scandinavian language family evolved from Old Scandinavian. Also called Old Norse, this parent tongue was established around AD 750, during the Viking expansion. Today, people speaking Danish, Norwegian, Swedish, or Icelandic understand much of each other's languages. Separate languages came into existence due to the lack of communication between groups of Vikings, as exploration led them in different directions.

Runic Swedish existed from 800 to 1225. The Vikings left glimpses into their culture in the form of runes, the earliest form of Germanic writing. The runic alphabet contained sixteen symbols, and people believed that

To the left is the Rök runestone, located in Östergötland, Sweden. The Rök runestone, dating from the Viking period, is covered with 800 runic letters, which have defied translation. On the right is a man reading a Swedish newspaper. Swedish is the official and most dominant language used in Sweden.

Approximately 160 daily newspapers cover the news of Swedish cities and countryside. As in the United States, freedom of press and freedom of speech are written into Swedish law.

they held magical significance. Engravers were highly respected because of their links to mystical powers. Much of our knowledge of the Swedish Viking tradition and history comes from runes carved on huge standing stones. These commonly contain public notices, records, and memorials. The Rök Stone in Östergötland is Sweden's most impressive, containing over 750 runes and conveying a wealth of information. Some of the intelligible fragments tell the story of an epic adventure, although scholars do not have the knowledge to translate the entire text.

Old Swedish evolved from Runic Swedish when the language incorporated the Latin alphabet. This form lasted until about 1550. The era of modern Swedish began with the first complete Swedish translation of the Bible, completed in 1541. Since then, contemporary Swedish has been further influenced by other languages. Swedish borrowed vocabulary from German when it was linked to the Hanseatic League and, like English, adopted many words derivative of Latin and French. In recent times, Sweden has imported many words directly from English. For example, modern Swedes listen to live *musik* and utilize the *internet*.

This has been a one-way exchange, since very few Swedish words have been accepted into English. One notable exception is the word and concept of "ombudsman," an official who looks into citizens' claims of mistreatment by public officials. Governmental ombudsmen deal with issues such as legislation, discrimination, and court decisions. Many corporations and schools both in Sweden and abroad also have ombudsmen who act as watchdogs and mediators. The ombudsman is a product of

King Magnus Eriksson, ruler of Sweden from 1319 to 1364, created a state law code, which superseded the provincial law code. Because of Magnus Eriksson's implementation of the state laws, he is responsible for laying the groundwork for a united Sweden. This painting from the National Law Codes of Magnus Eriksson, which is part of the Uppsala University Collection, Sweden/Bridgeman Art Library, is a gruesome depiction of crime.

Helpful Swedish Words

English	Swedish	Swedish pronunciation
Hello	Hej	hay
	God dag (formal)	goo dahg
Goodbye	Hej då	hey do
Yes/No	Ja/Nej	yah/nay
Please	Varsågod	vahr-shaw-good
Thank you	Tack	tack
Sorry	Ursäkta	oor-shehk-tah
I don't know.	Jag vet inte.	yah vayt in-teh
What is your name?	Jag heter du?	yah hay-ter dew
My name is	Jag heter	yah hay-ter
I don't speak Swedish.	Jag talar inte svenska.	yah tah-lar in-teh sven-skah
Do you speak English?	Talar du engelska?	ta-lar doo en-yel-ska
What time is it?	Hur mycket är klockan?	hewr mew-keh ay klock-a
Help!	Hjälp!	yelp
I'm lost.	Jag har tappat bort mig.	yah har tap-pat bort may
How do I get to . . .?	Kan Ni visa mig vägen till . . .?	kahn nee vee-sah may vay-gehn teel
House	Hus	hoos
Restaurant	Restaurang	res-tawr-rang
Bathroom	Toaletten	twah-leht-en
Car	Bil	beel
1	Ett	ett
2	Två	tvaw
3	Tre	tray
4	Fyra	few-ra
5	Fem	fem

the Swedes' active social conscience, and of a government concerned with treating its citizens with fairness and justice.

Beginners in the language will discover that Swedish uses the same alphabet as English, although each letter has a precise pronunciation. Most are pronounced the same in every context, although newcomers may be confused by occasional silent

The Swedish Language: From Ancient Swedish to Modern Swedish

People walk the street of Österlänggatan in Stockholm's Gamla Stan. Known as the Cradle of Stockholm, Gamla Stan is the most popular attraction in Stockholm.

consonants such as "g" and "j." Three additional vowels—å, ä, and ö—increase the number of letters in the alphabet to twenty-nine. These are considered separate letters from "a" and "o" and occur at the end of the alphabet. Therefore, a student looking for information on the island of Öland must hunt under the last letter listed in an index. Native Swedish vocabulary does not include "q", "w", or "z." A few sounds are uniquely Swedish, and English speakers find them difficult to reproduce. For example, the closest equivalent to the "sj" sound is "sh," or "ch" as in "loch." Some Swedish nouns are gendered: descriptive articles and adjectives vary depending on whether the word is "common" or "neutral." In earlier forms of Swedish, nouns required different articles depending on whether they were masculine, feminine, or neutral. In modern Swedish, masculine and feminine nouns are combined into a "common" grouping.

Spoken Swedish has a singing quality, with the pitch rising and falling more than in English. To the Swedes, English sounds flat. Swedish dialects vary from one region to the next, but these differences have diminished in modern times. Most Swedes speak some English, which has been required in schools for many years. A small number of Swedish citizens consider Swedish their second language. This includes at least 300,000 Finnish speakers, most living on the border of Finland. Different Samish groups within Sweden speak four different languages, although most also speak and write Swedish. These Samish languages belong to the Finno-Ugric family of languages, unrelated to the Germanic languages. The Samish languages have an extensive vocabulary describing natural conditions in the Arctic Circle, including over one hundred words for snow. The word "tundra" is of Sami origin. A small Roma population speaks Vlax Romani, kin to many Central European languages. Sweden's population has become more diverse due to post–World War II immigration, but non-Swedish speakers still remain a small minority.

SWEDISH MYTHS AND LEGENDS

4

or centuries Swedes have shivered and laughed at well-spun tales handed down through the ages. Many of Sweden's myths and traditions go back to the Viking days, when men explored the seas and fought battles to please their gods. Others reach only as far as the backyard, where fairies or sprites still frolic through the night. The gods battle fierce trolls, witches fly across the horizon, and dwarves mine the mountains in search of gems and precious metals.

Viking Lore

Viking tales describe the structure and intrigues of the religious pantheon. These stories explained the natural world, offered social insights, and also—perhaps most importantly—provided entertainment for the long nights of winter. Though Viking mythology spread throughout Scandinavia, the tradition was probably strongest in Sweden. A wide variety of creatures and gods inhabited this fantastic universe. The gods, despite their powers and attributes, lived much as humans did. They fought, feasted, loved, and killed. Their honor and courage served as an example for their worshipers, who took the lessons of the gods to heart.

At the center of the Viking universe grew a giant ash tree named Yggdrasil. Rising through all space and time, the mighty ash's branches spanned the skies over heaven and earth. A well called Mimir rose from the ground at its base, containing the waters of wisdom and understanding. Each of Yggdrasil's three roots passes through a different world, binding the universe together. Asgard, the land of the gods, hosts one root. Another passes through

This section of Viking tapestry *(left)*, dating from the twelfth century, shows the three most important Viking gods. Odin is the god of war. Thor is the god of thunder. Freyr, carrying an axe, a hammer, and an ear of corn, is the god of fertility. On the right is a bronze amulet dating from the Viking period of the ninth century. It portrays a man wearing a horned helmet and holding a sword and two spears. He represents a priest of the cult of Odin. Both artifacts are located at the Statens Historiska Museet in Stockholm, Sweden.

This illustration is from a document called *Eddalaeren* by Finn Magnusen. Dated 1824, it represents Magnusen's idea of Yggdrassil from Viking myth. The evergreen ash tree found throughout Viking mythology is said to overshadow the entire universe.

Jotunheim, where the frost giants dwell. The third binds them to Niflheim, a world of mists and shadows occupied by the dead and ruled by the goddess Hel.

Midgard, the world of man, rests halfway up Yggdrasil's trunk. When time began, a frost giant named Ymir emerged from the ice that bound the universe. The first man and woman grew from under his left arm, and hid in the trunk of Yggdrasil to await the end of the world. The frost giants emerged from his feet. Ymir had a son named Bor, who in turn had three children, the gods Odin, Vili, and Ve. The three of them slew the old frost giant, and formed the earth from his body. They created a population of humans from trees, and also the dwarves, small and stout people who lived beneath the earth and crafted treasures from the metals they mined.

The gods and goddesses belonged to a race of beings called the Aesir, who controlled the fate of all other creatures. Odin the All-Father was their leader and reigned over Asgard, their legendary realm. Odin sacrificed an eye for the privilege of drinking from Mimir. The wisest of the gods, he was also the fiercest. Warriors slain in battle came to Valhalla, his great hall in Asgard. There they spend eternity feasting and fighting.

Odin's eldest son was Thor, the god of thunder. He was the strongest of all the gods, and wielded the hammer Mjollnir, a great weapon crafted by the dwarves for slaying giants. He thundered through the skies in a chariot pulled by goats, Mjollnir striking its targets like lightning before returning to his hand.

Ragnarok

The Vikings believed that the world would end in the aftermath of a cataclysmic battle called Ragnarok. The battle follows a period of increasing turmoil throughout the universe. All bound monsters break free, wars and strife occur amongst humanity, and the armies of the giants assemble for a final assault against the gods. Loki leads these masses into the battle. Each of the Aesir engages a monster or giant, and each pair battles to the death. In the end, all the gods and monsters fall dead, the  wolf Fenris swallows the sun, and Asgard, Midgard, and Jotunheim are consumed by fire. Only Yggdrasil and the man and woman hidden inside the world tree's trunk survive the catastrophe. When the destruction ends, they are to leave their shelter and step out into a fresh, renewed Earth, giving humanity a new start. Asgard is also restored, with the children of the gods destroyed at Ragnarok taking care of the universe. In taking the world from total destruction to total renewal, the tale of Ragnarok offers both a warning and hope to humanity.

The fertility deities Freya, Freyr, and Njord brought harvests and good fortune to the faithful. Njord governed the seas and the winds, helping sailors and fishermen. Freyr, Njord's son, gave the world sunshine and rain. Freyja was the goddess of love and death. She rode upon a chariot pulled by cats, and welcomed fallen warriors to her hall just as Odin did.

Balder, the god of light and joy, was Odin's second son. A kind, just, poetic, and wise deity, Balder was the most beloved by humans and other gods. At one point, all things

The witch hunts of Sweden began in Dalarna, where the first trial took place in 1668. These trials lasted until 1677, and during this time approximately 200 people were executed. This photograph was taken in Njupan Creek in Dalarna, Sweden, an area synonymous with witchcraft.

living and nonliving took an oath never to harm him. Only the mistletoe plant did not take the oath, the gods considering it too insignificant to ask.

Loki, the trickster, was the most cunning and malicious resident of Asgard. The son of a giant, he both helped and hindered the Aesir. He tricked Balder's blind brother, Hoder, god of darkness, into throwing a dart tipped with mistletoe. Guided by Loki's hand, the dart struck Balder dead. The furious Aesir captured Loki and chained him to a rock, where he remains until the end of the world.

Magic and Superstition

When Christianity became powerful in Sweden during the twelfth century and drove the lore of the gods into the shadows, new traditions emerged. Fireside whispers turned from the escapades of Freyja and Balder to the trickery of witches, sprites, and spirits. Most villages had a resident capable of magic, for the right price. The Klocka man lived on the fringe of Swedish society and claimed the ability to cure those made ill by trolls and other magical beings.

Magical practices were so widely accepted in medieval Sweden that the Riksdag passed laws forbidding *maleficium*, or harmful magic. The church later outlawed divinations, exorcisms, pacts with the devil, and incantations of any sort. Punishments for those caught practicing magic ranged from banishment to death. The forbidden nature of witchcraft spawned many stories and rumors, going far beyond the Klocka man's benevolent powers. Any ill fortune was instantly blamed on the witches who seemed to be peeping around every corner. Their numbers were said to darken the skies overhead as they flew to the legendary black mountain Blakullå for their meetings and ceremonies, headed by the devil himself.

At the top of the full-page illustration, the German inscription reads, "Picture of the gruesome Witches deeds and unbelievable Devilish temptations in the Kingdom of Sweden, but especially occurring with the inhabitants of the Village of Mohra. In the Year 1670." This image comes from a German text dated at the end of the seventeenth century that describes the witch trials in Sweden.

The stone carving, which dates from the late Viking period, depicts the Viking god Loki, god of mischief. It shows Loki's head with his lips sewn shut. The carving is housed at the Aarhus Art Museum in Aarhus, Denmark.

Irrational fears of witches grew particularly strong in the late 1500s, when hundreds of people were executed and many more put on trial for practicing witchcraft. Most were brought before the courts solely on the testimony of imaginative children, but fearful adults were always quick to back up their claims. Though the witch hunt craze fell off by the late 1600s, people were put on trial for practicing magic well into the eighteenth century.

Other Legends

Popular folktales deal with foolish or unlucky characters, and most Swedes laugh long and hard at their silliness. Light-spirited in tone, many resemble children's fairy tales told all around the world. The popular story "The Princess of Catburg" is very similar to "Puss in Boots." Both feature characters from humble beginnings who end up enormously wealthy thanks to the hard work of a sharp-witted cat.

Created by an unnamed artist, this illustration first appeared in the June 23, 1918, issue of *Allers Familj-Journal* in Sweden. In the drawing, older witches stir a magic potion while younger witches dance around the cauldron during midsummer's night in Sweden.

Famous Swedish artist John Bauer (1882–1918) created this illustration to accompany the fairy tale *The Sorceress and the Royal Children*.

A host of sinister and weird creatures populate Swedish folk stories. Most involve some sort of spirit, playing tricks on hapless people wandering into their territories. *Skogsrå* are forest spirits who watch over all the plants and animals within their range. Though they look like hollow tree trunks from the back, their fronts resemble beautiful women. These unpredictable spirits bless those they favor, and have fun at the expense of everyone else. Farmers whose cattle wander into the woods and lost travelers often blame the Skogsrå, while successful mushroom pickers thank them. *Nisse* are household spirits who look after a family's home and livestock in exchange for a place to rest and occasional gifts. Usually helpful, they can cause trouble when angered or slighted.

Sprites populate Sweden's emptier spots, giving many lone wanderers something to talk about once they're safely inside. *Näcken*, water sprites, sit in deep waters and play the violin, calling victims in to drown with beautiful music. After the sun goes down, the fairies emerge and dance to the music of the Näcken violins, causing trouble for any who interrupt their fun. Far from these festivities, *Lyktgubbe* travel the countryside as mischievous little old men. On dark nights they like to shine their lanterns toward the road, drawing the curious away from their destinations until they are hopelessly lost. Occasionally they help lost people escape from danger, guiding them back to safety by the light of their lamps.

Trolls have occupied a place in Swedish folklore since the Viking days. These large-footed, slow-witted, lumbering creatures live under rocks and in caves, hiding from daylight. Few ever see them, and they are rumored to have the power to become invisible. They love gold and wealth of any kind, amassing legendary treasure troves. Those foolish enough to go seeking troll treasure often vanish mysteriously, though occasionally their well-gnawed bones turn up in some remote place.

SWEDISH FESTIVALS AND CEREMONIES OF ANTIQUITY AND TODAY

5

Sweden's holiday traditions come from a combination of ancient pagan lore and official Church practices. Many of the celebrations originated from folk tradition and emphasize family and community ties. The Swedish may bring out special costumes and decorations, display national or regional flags, prepare traditional foods, and engage in festivities enjoyed for generations. International influences, especially Germanic, have had an impact on native customs.

The Swedes consider Easter an important holiday, second only to Christmas. Anticipation begins more than a month before, on Shrove Tuesday. The Swedes eat *Semlor* buns on this day and all subsequent Tuesdays of Lent. These yummy pastries are filled with marzipan and cream, dusted with powdered sugar, and served in a dish of hot milk. The Easter break gives families a chance to clean the house and yard and maybe even check on their boats or visit the country. Homes are decorated in Easter pastels, spring flowers, and *påskris*, birch twigs ornamented with feathers.

On the left are three young girls dressed as Easter Witches. In Sweden, children dress up as Easter Witches on the Thursday before Easter and travel from house to house giving Easter cards in exchange for gifts or money. Above, Swedish actors at the Skoklosterspelen (Skokloster Pageant) are dressed as medieval royalty. During this pageant, the three epochs in Sweden's history are shown on stage: the Middle Ages, Sweden's golden age (seventeenth century), and the turn of the twentieth century.

Here are people in Stockholm on Walpurgis Night. People today celebrate Walpurgis Night in much the same way as the Vikings, who began this tradition. Crowds of people gather around bonfires and sing songs to welcome the return of spring.

Folklore tells that witches traveled to the dark mountain Blåkulla on Maundy Thursday to meet with the devil. Modern "witches" and "hoboes" dress up in gaudy, ragged costumes on the Thursday or Saturday before Easter, and go from house to house asking for sweets and coins in exchange for Easter cards. Almost all Swedes attend the Easter Sunday church service. Many paint and hunt for Easter eggs, and light a bonfire or fireworks.

April 30 is *Valborgmässoafton*, or Walpurgis Night, when Swedes hail the return of spring with bonfires and other festivities. This holiday is particularly popular with university students of Uppsala and Lund, and recent *gymnasieskolan* graduates just completing the Swedish equivalent of high school. Many wear their white graduation caps, as Walpurgis Night coincides with traditional student celebrations.

On June 6, National Day, Swedes raise their flags and attend speeches and parades. Gustav Vasa became the first Swedish king on this date in 1523, and the

Riksdag enacted a new constitution in 1809. Swedes first observed the holiday in 1916.

Midsummer's Eve marks the beginning of summer, celebrated on the weekend closest to the solstice. Children decorate the towering *majstäng*, or midsummer pole, with wreaths, greenery, and flowers. Family and friends gather in the country, sometimes in national clothing, for dancing, music, games, and food long into the night.

The Christmas season begins with Advent, four Sundays before Christmas. Every week an Advent candle is lit, so that four candles are burning for Christmas Day. On December 13, Saint Lucia Day, the youngest daughter of a household brings her family morning coffee, *Lussekatter* or "Lucia cats" (saffron buns), and *pepparkakor* (ginger cookies). She wears a long, white robe tied with a red sash and a crown of tall candles on her head, and sings traditional songs. The day continues as processions of Lucias and her attendants pay visits to places such as churches, hospitals, workplaces, and schools. "Star boys" also participate, wearing pointed hats and carrying

Attended by Royalty

Sweden's monarch no longer wields any power in the government, but the royal family still holds the attention and respect of the people. Any event gains a bit of prestige by the appearance of a royal. King Carl XVI Gustav performs a number of formal public duties each year, such as the opening of the Riksdag's session and officiating at the Nobel Ceremony. When the Öresund Link was completed, Crown Princess Victoria met Crown Prince Frederik of Denmark at the center of the bridge only hours after the last block of the bridge fell into place.

In the early morning hours of December 13, young girls dress in traditional white gowns with red sashes and crowns of lingonberry twigs. They carry candles. Walking from house to house, they brings baked goods. This festival of lights is held on St. Lucia's feast day.

star wands. This is a beloved, uniquely Swedish holiday. Many communities elect their own Lucia, and there is even a national Lucia of the year!

The Swedes decorate with Advent stars, Christmas trees, and red tulips. Christmas Eve is the traditional day of celebration. Families spend the afternoon watching cartoons, including "Donald Duck's Christmas," and share a huge meal. Afterward, a family member dresses up as the *tomte*, or Christmas gnome, and hands out presents. On Christmas Day, everyone rises early for the early *julottan*, the Christmas church service. The julottan is candlelit and ends before dawn. The Christmas season concludes on *Knut*, January 13. Families take down decorations and gobble up any remaining Christmas treats.

The Sami market in Jokkmokk, Sweden, which has the qualities of a winter festival, serves as an occasion for the Sami people to trade and socialize. The Jokkmokk market is an attraction where both Sami people and tourists enjoy concerts, slide shows, lectures, and winter activities.

Sweden's most popular tradition is the raising of the maypole on Midsummer's Day. Celebrations include dressing the maypole with birch leaves and flowers, followed by games and dancing.

New Year's celebrations resemble those in the United States: fireworks, parties, and champagne late into the night. Many families set off their own stockpile of fireworks.

Children celebrate birthdays with parties and cake. Some parents still follow the old tradition of serving children breakfast in bed.

Regional Events

Sweden's annual regional events bring participants from across the country, as well as international visitors. The diversity of these occasions show the Swedes' wide variety of interests and pastimes. Many are related to sports and the outdoors; others celebrate music and the arts. Stockholm, the country's cultural center

Alfred Nobel (1833–1896) was born in Stockholm, Sweden, into a family of engineers. In 1866, at the age of thirty-three, Nobel unknowingly invented dynamite. Nobel had many other inventions, holding 350 patents. However, Nobel is best known for the nine-million-dollar endowment he left in his will to create an annual Nobel Prize. He was inspired to reward efforts on behalf of peace and humanity after inadvertently giving the world a weapon of war.

53

as well as its capital, hosts numerous events. The Orient Festival introduces a weekend of Arabic culture in June. Directors from all over the world bring innovative films to the Stockholm International Film Festival in November. December 10 is the Nobel Prize ceremony, founded by the scientist and inventor Alfred Nobel. The Nobel Foundation recognizes great achievers in chemistry, physics, medicine, literature, and economics, and awards the prestigious Peace Prize. The ceremony is followed by the social event of the year: a banquet in the opulent Blå Hallen (Blue Hall) of the Stadhuset, Stockholm's City Hall.

During the first weekend of February, the Sami hold a market at Jokkmokk. They exhibit traditional handicrafts,

This last will and testament of Alfred Nobel established the Nobel Prize for the future. Nobel requested that cash prizes be awarded in the areas of physics, chemistry, medicine, literature, and peace to those who contribute to the common good of humanity. The first Nobel Prize ceremony took place in 1901 on the fifth anniversary of Nobel's death.

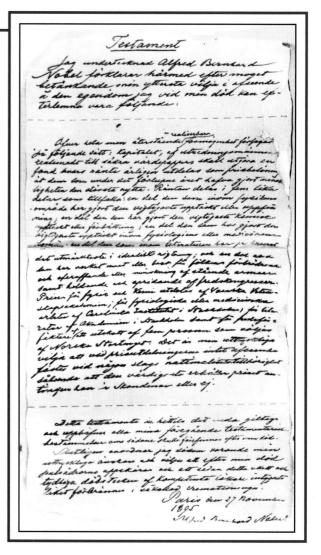

such as woodcarvings and textiles, and hold reindeer races. In August, the history-rich island of Visby is transported back to the Middle Ages for Medieval Week. People in period dress reenact medieval trade, theater, and music, with everything from the antics of the court fool to jousting tournaments. Later in the month is Minnesota Day at Växjö, the town were many nineteenth-century Swedes boarded the boat for America, often ending up in the Midwest. Swedish-Americans return on this day to celebrate their heritage.

THE RELIGIONS OF SWEDEN THROUGHOUT ITS HISTORY

6

Like the glaciers that formed and shaped the land many millions of years ago, the religions of Sweden have changed throughout the centuries. Slow, steady pressure built up to abrupt and even violent shifts in faiths, as the Swedes tested traditions before moving on to a new interpretation of life and eternity. Though the Viking beliefs and Roman Catholicism were ultimately discarded and the Lutheran Church of Sweden was finally separated from the state, echoes of each faith still resonate today in runes and traditions. Even some days of the week take their names from the Viking gods: Wednesday (*Onsdag* in Swedish) for Odin, Thursday (*Torsdag*) for Thor, and Friday (*Fredag*) for Freya.

Old Scandinavian Religion

The Scandinavian tradition grew out of earth-based polytheistic faiths practiced by the various tribes that settled in Sweden around 10,000 BC. These evolved into a complex pantheon of gods and goddesses by the time of the Vikings. Rune stones, sagas, and old poems outline the significance of Yggdrassil, Ragnarok, Valhalla, and the adventures of the Viking deities. The Vikings left behind a wealth of information regarding their beliefs, but very little evidence describes their religious practices. They made sacrifices to their gods, offering animals, items, and sometimes human

The photograph on the left was taken September 12, 2001, in the Dome of Lund at a service for the September 11 victims in the United States. Churches throughout Sweden held services on this day. Above is a pendant dating from Sweden's Viking period, which is housed in Statens Historiska Museet in Stockholm, Sweden. The pendant depicts Freya, the goddess of love and death. Here Freya wears a necklace named Brisingamen made for her by the dwarves, which prevented men or gods from withstanding her charms.

De facris, & facrificiis Gothorum.

Drawn by Olaus Magnus in 1555 for his book *Historia gentibus septentrional- ibus*, the illustration portrays priests and others watching as victims are burned in ancient Scandinavia. The one original copy of this book that survives is housed in the Munich State Library in Munich, Germany.

beings in exchange for bountiful harvests, good sailing winds, and success in battle. Warriors returned home after profitable campaigns to make their battle sacrifices, thanking the gods for their help with gifts of captives, horses, and weapons. People occupying coastal areas all over Europe trembled before fierce Viking raiders, and so naturally assumed their religion to be just as bloodthirsty as their business practices. Much of the fearsome reputation surrounding Viking religion came from the testimony of priests and monks whose coastal abbeys and monasteries were often raided as a convenient way to get supplies and trade goods.

Vikings favored empty hilltops as sites for sacrifices or rituals. Unique rock formations and certain kinds of trees enhanced a location's power, indicating a mark left by the gods. Runes, standing stones, and occasional artifacts show that these spots were frequently used. Priests and people gifted with special powers or connections to the gods guided the ceremonies, taking every step possible to avoid angering the gods. In towns and settlements, rituals took place in public temples. Central to the Viking faith was the temple at Uppsala, where the highest-ranking priests presided. There, at the largest temple in Sweden, it was said that the streets ran red with the blood of sacrifices on holy days.

Before the days of the Vikings, people buried their dead in barrows, great mounds constructed of earth and stone with room inside for a body. Vikings continued the practice, as it gave them ample space for supplying the dead with provisions needed in the afterlife. Viking myths tell that warriors who fell in battle were picked up by Odin's Valkyries—armored maidens astride winged horses—and brought to Asgard to live in Valhalla. Weapons, armor, valuables, and talismans accompanied fallen warriors to the grave to prepare them for this raucous afterlife. Many were buried in boats or a barrow marked by stones arranged in a ship's outline. Those who died of old age, sickness, or by accident went to

Niflheim, the world of mists and shadows. The journey was a long and difficult one for a spirit, and bodies were buried with food, clothing, and any items that might help them along on the trip.

Missionaries and Catholicism

Sweden kept its polytheistic faith longer than the other Scandinavian countries, despite missionaries' continuous efforts to convert the country. Frankish missionaries led by Saint Angsar landed in Sweden in AD 829, intending to stop Viking raids by introducing Christianity to the Swedes. The Swedish kings, who all claimed to be descendents of Odin, welcomed them warmly and allowed them free passage throughout the country, but few

The Hammer of Thor

Many Viking warriors wore a necklace bearing a representation of Mjollnir, Thor's legendary hammer. Roughly two inches long with a hole in the "handle," these talismans were hung from a string or chain with the hammer's "head" pointing downward. The handle extended slightly beyond the head, and another hole was drilled into it near the bottom. When the Viking ships sailed into Christian ports, they turned the hammers upside-down, hanging them through the bottom holes to resemble crucifixes. If anyone refused to trade with the Vikings because they did not believe in Christianity, the Norsemen could point to their "crucifixes" as evidence of conversion!

Swedes adopted Christianity. The Catholic Church sent scores of missionaries over the next couple centuries, but made little headway. During the eleventh century, the Christians won a major victory when the Swedish king Olaf Skottkonung converted to the Christian faith. More Swedes warmed to Christianity, but many allowed it as either a belief parallel with the old gods or rejected it outright. Standing stones dating from the period sometimes show Christian iconography next to symbols of the Viking gods. Since Christian ports refused to trade with

Above is the Gannarve Stoneship located in Gotland, Sweden. During the Viking Age, Gotland was the major trade center of northern Europe. Many stoneships have been found to be burial mounds. Some are thought to be for a chieftan or trader. About half of the 20,000 Viking age silver coins currently in existence have been found in Gotland.

pagans, seafarers learned to profess knowledge and acceptance of a single god.

Catholicism eventually prevailed over paganism through sheer persistence. King Inge, an early Christian Swedish ruler, demolished the temple at Uppsala in the twelfth century and built a church over its ruins to symbolize the end of the old religion. Sweden began crusading against Finland under King Erik IX during the twelfth century. Religious raids continued off and on under different rulers for the next two centuries until Sweden absorbed Finland and forced an end to paganism in that country.

Erik IX became the first patron saint of Sweden. He was killed in 1160 while worshipping in Uppsala shortly after returning from his crusade. Laid to rest at Old Uppsala Cathedral in 1220, his remains attracted many pilgrims, once again resembling the old pagan temple during its busiest times. Saint Bridget, another patron saint of Sweden, founded the Bridgettine Order. A mother of eight, after

This illustration of the German bishop Ansgar appears in the book *Overland, Norges Historie*, whose author is unknown. Bishop Ansgar is an important figure in Swedish ecclesiastical history because he introduced Christianity to Sweden in 829.

the death of her husband she followed a lifelong series of visions from God and founded a monastic order. Intended as a model for the reformation of religious orders, its sisters followed a very strict code of behavior dedicated to assisting any person in need. Bridget moved to Rome in 1349 and spent the remainder of her life far from her native country.

While heroes and saints helped Catholicism win followers, connections to the monarchy made the church a mighty institution. The Clergy emerged as one of the four social classes under the rule of Mangus Laduläs during the late thirteenth century, setting them as political equals to the nobility, farmers, and merchants. Monarchs stripped land from the nobles, ceding it to the church tax-free. Special privileges granted by the crown gave the church more and more freedom from authority, until it became very wealthy and powerful. By the sixteenth century, the Catholic Church owned almost a fifth of the land in Sweden and operated independently of the Riksdag and the Crown.

Carved in 1160 inside the tomb of Swedish King Eric IX, this engraving depicts a scene of death by beheading. According to history, King Eric IX died at the hands of a Danish prince. In 1290, he became the patron saint of Sweden as Eric the Saint.

Located in Uppsala Cathedral in Uppsala, Sweden, this alfresco painting illustrates Swedish King Gustav Vasa receiving a Bible translation in 1451 from Olaus Petri and Laurentius Andre. Under Gustav Vasa, the country became Protestant, making him head of state instead of the pope.

The Reformation and Lutheranism

The Reformation of the church, a movement started by Martin Luther in 1517 in Germany, focused on taking Christianity out of the hands of powerful and corrupt church officials and giving it directly to the people. The movement arrived in Sweden in the 1520s. King Gustav Vasa saw the religious shift as a perfect opportunity to regain property and authority from the Catholic Church. In 1527 he confiscated and sold much of the church's holdings to the nobility in order to pay Sweden's gigantic debts. He also brought the church under his control, ending its autonomy. Lutheranism officially replaced Catholicism as the national religion in 1529 with the appointment of several Lutherans to high church office, making Sweden a Protestant state.

Lutherans believe the Bible to be the only authority on God and that only grace can save humanity from evil. When Sweden adopted Lutheranism, one of Vasa's first actions was to have the Bible and other religious texts translated from Latin to Swedish. Likewise, all church services and ceremonies were performed in Swedish. Church events offered opportunities to socialize with neighbors, as well as special classes and activities in the evenings. The Church also provided an education for Swedish children, teaching them how to read and write before public schools appeared during the 1840s. While not as powerful as the old Catholic Church, Lutheran clergy still served as one of the four ruling estates of Sweden until that system disappeared in 1866.

The image on the panel to the left was painted in oil during the late fifteenth century. It depicts Christ appearing to Saint Bridget. She was a Swedish widow who became a saint on October 7, 1391, because of her visions since age seven of Christ's crucifixion.

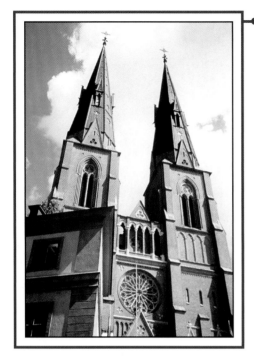

This cathedral, located in Uppsala, Sweden, is the oldest and largest in the country. Construction of the Uppsala Cathedral began in the eleventh century on the site of an old pagan temple and took nearly 175 years to complete.

Swedish Religion Today

Modern churches hold services once a week and focus heavily on the sermon given by clergy. Every church receives a copy of the *Evangeliebok*, or *Book of the Gospels*, containing sermons for every Sunday and Holy Day, along with alternate sermons. One of these must be read every week in every church, keeping all of the congregations in Sweden more or less on the same page throughout the year. The ruling monarch may pick four special days of prayer, where every sermon in every church comes from the same text. The chief service is called High Mass, and is generally a simple affair consisting of little more than the sermon. Congregations sometimes take Communion, though it does not serve a central role in the church service and many do not even perform the ritual annually. Parishioners may choose to attend either a morning or evening prayer session in addition to the High Mass.

The church is headed by bishops, with the archbishopric centered at Uppsala. Priests serve individual congregations, sometimes with the help of deacons or young priests. Most of Sweden's deacons concentrate mainly on community services rather than administration. True to Sweden's spirit of equality, women make up a large portion of the clergy.

According to the Svenska Institute, 95 percent of Swedes regularly attended church up until the middle of the twentieth century, but today most Swedes are indifferent toward religious practices. Church attendance has dropped further since the early 1990s and few Swedes regularly make it to High Mass, although most still hold church weddings, funerals, and confirmations. Though 86 percent belong to the Swedish Church, less than 10 percent regularly attend services.

Freedom of religion has been an active concept in Sweden since the eighteenth century, but was not a legally guaranteed right until 1951. Up until 1994, everyone

Visby, Sweden, is a medieval city revered for its ruins and stone architecture. A wall encloses the oldest part. Every August, Visby revisits its heritage by staging a medieval week that takes participants back to the year 1361.

born in Sweden automatically became a Church member and remained one unless the person formally withdrew. Today, only the monarch and the minister in charge of church affairs have to belong to the Church. In January 2000, the Riksdag eliminated government funding for the Church. Beginning in 1985, children learn about all the religions of the world in the classroom, instead of just studying Christianity and the Church of Sweden. These reforms have brought about a separation of church and state despite Sweden retaining Lutheranism as the official religion.

Though the majority of native Swedes are Lutheran by default, other religions are slowly gaining followers. Roman Catholicism, other Protestant branches, Judaism, Islam, and Hinduism have grown in numbers across Sweden as people from other cultures immigrate to the country. In recent years, these immigrants, wanting their children to grow up with their own faith, lobbied for many of the policy changes guaranteeing religious freedom.

To the north, the Sami also practice their own faith. Most Sami officially belong to the Church of Sweden, but a few still adhere to the nature-based religion of their ancestors. Certain places of power take on meaning within the Samish tradition, much like the Viking faith. Shamans interact with spiritual gods and ancestors with the help of drums, sacred items, and special rituals. The faithful make offerings to these beings in exchange for health and good fortune. Everyone has their own set of ancestors and believes in their own gods, making the Samish faith deeply personal. A person's *joik*, or "song of the plains," conveys his or her spiritual essence in a personal melody.

THE ART AND ARCHITECTURE OF SWEDEN

7

Asurvey of Swedish architecture gives a sense of Sweden's long history and rapid development through the past century. Sweden's cities have winding medieval lanes just down the block from modern skyscrapers. Villagers take for granted Middle Age carvings in their churches and anecdotes of local Viking adventures that took place a millennium past. Gamla Stan, Stockholm's Old Town,

nestles on two small islands at the heart of the city, where structures dating from the thirteenth century still stand. Sigtuna, Sweden's oldest town, was founded in the tenth century, although the "modern" city hall and tourist office both date from the 1700s. UNESCO, the United Nations Educational, Scientific and Cultural Organization, named nine locations in Sweden as official World Heritage sites, including the town of Visby in Gotland.

It has served as a useful trading stop since prehistoric times, and Gotland, or "home of the Goths," is scattered with Viking and prehistoric sites as well as dozens of medieval churches.

Artist Anders Leonhard Zorn (1860–1920) is famous for his paintings of the people of Dalarna. The 1897 oil, shown on the left, depicts Swedes performing a traditional country folk dance on Midsummer's Eve. Above is an aerial view of the Gamla Stan district in Stockholm, Sweden. Located at the entrance to Lake Mälaren, it dates from the thirteenth century, making it the most historic district in Stockholm.

One of Sweden's most popular historical sites is the city wall of Visby. This medieval structure, built in the late thirteenth century, was at one time connected to the Castle of Visborg. The castle was an impenetrable stronghold, complete with towers, moats, and a stone wall to guard against invaders.

Although Sweden is proud of its long policy of neutrality, remnants of city walls and the many fortresses on strategic coastlines and islands attest to a long, warlike past. A fifth-century Iron Age fortress guarded the southeastern island of Öland from raiders. A Norwegian ruler built the fourteenth-century Bohus Fortress to defend his southern border from Sweden, but the Swedes gained the territory anyway through treaties and later used the fortress as a prison. The Carlston Fortress overlooks the resort island of Marstrand on Sweden's west coast. Karl X Gustav ordered its construction in the 1660s after seizing Marstrand from the Danes.

Old castles and mansions, many open to the public, abound in the southern half of Sweden. The southernmost province of Skåne is known as the "chateau district" and dates to the days when the nobility demonstrated their prestige by erecting opulent residences. Many of the most impressive buildings were constructed for members of the royal family.

Kalmar Castle, constructed in the 1200s, played a vital role in the 1397 union of Kalmud. In the sixteenth century, the Vasas rebuilt it in a Renaissance style. Kungliga Slottet, the Royal Palace on Gamla Stan in Stockholm, was designed by Nicodemus Tessin in 1697. Completed in 1754, it contains 608 rooms and displays many artifacts of the monarchy throughout the centuries. Nearby are the thirteenth-century Storkyrkan and Riddarholmskyrkan,

The Royal Warship *Vasa*

In 1626, King Gustavus Adolphus commissioned the renowned Dutch shipbuilder Henrik Hybertsson to build a mighty ship that would lead the Swedish Navy to victories in the Thirty Years' War. Christened the *Vasa*, the finished vessel was the largest and most powerful ship in the world. Ornate carvings covered its exterior, and sixty-four guns nested on its two decks. The ship was a magnificent sight as it glided into the water on August 10, 1628. Minutes after the launch, the ship fired a salute, promptly capsized, and sank. In 1961, Sweden salvaged the ship from the bottom of Stockholm harbor. Still intact after 333 years underwater, it is the only surviving seventeenth-century ship in the world. Over seven hundred intricate wood carvings and ornaments were reassembled like a puzzle. Scientists continue looking for ways to preserve the wood from decay, so that this rare glimpse into earlier times can be studied and admired for years to come.

Stockholm's Cathedral, and the Riddarholm (Isle of the Knights) Church. Most of Sweden's monarchs lie entombed in Riddarholmskyrkan, once a Franciscan monastery. Today, King Karl XVI Gustav and his family reside at the Drottningholm Palace, a seventeenth-century "Versailles of Sweden," just outside Stockholm, also designed by Nicodemus Tessin.

Sweden's best-kept Renaissance castle or "the Key to the Realm," is the Kalmar Castle in Kalmar, Sweden. Begun in the twelfth century as a fortified tower, its strategic position at the border of Denmark and Sweden led to its further development. By the mid-fourteenth century it had become the strongest castle in northern Sweden. Renovations that created the structure as it stands today were begun in 1535 under the authority of King Gustav Vasa and his sons, Erik XIV and Johan III, each of whom made extensive changes. The last monarch to live and work in Kalmar Castle was King Carl XI from 1673 to 1692.

Swedish peasants once lived in brightly painted wooden farmhouses. Until the twentieth century, much of the population occupied small villages in the countryside, but new agricultural and industrial practices forced them toward urban areas. Because Sweden's Industrial Revolution began late, and early industry centered around mining and timber, the urban population did not outnumber the rural until the 1930s. Urban planners and architects worked together to guide the development of Sweden's cities. They combined simple and rustic styles with international designs familiar to Swedes.

The Swedish people felt a sense of national pride and optimism for the future, and welcomed the progressive new buildings. Stockholm's Stadhuset, or city hall, built in 1923, is the greatest architectural creation of this transitional period. Designed by the National Romantic School of

Gunnar Asplund (1885–1940) holds an important place in the history of modern architecture. Hailed as Stockholm's master builder, Asplund was the dominant architect of the 1920s, his work representing Scandinavian Classicism, also known as Swedish Grace.

Architecture architect Ragnar Ostberg, it is a modern, red-brick structure with an elegant interior used for state functions and the Nobel Prize banquet. Sweden's most renowned architect, Gunnar Asplund (1885–1940) worked at this time. He developed some of the ideals of functionalism and designed many public buildings such as courthouses and libraries.

Today, most Swedes live in the outskirts and suburbs of large towns and cities. More people occupy apartment buildings than single-family residences. Urban planning included spacious streets and ample green space, so the urban population density is less than in most cities. Over 50 percent of Sweden's homes were built after 1960, in a construction boom that peaked in 1970. Most housing is sturdy and well insulated, with a simple interior design and plenty of natural light. Swedes tend to furnish their homes sparingly with a combination of sleek modern design and traditional rustic decorations.

This building is the Stadsbiblioteket, Stockholm's city library, designed by Swedish architect Gunnar Asplund. It was completed in 1928. This photograph was taken circa 1930.

The Icehotel

Swedes suffering from cabin fever through the long winter can leave town to spend a weekend at the famous Icehotel in Jukkasjärvi, 125 miles (201.2 kilometers) inside the Arctic Circle. Essentially a huge igloo built entirely from ice and steel supports, the unheated hotel has attracted thousands of guests annually since its inception in 1993. Every year, owner Yngve Bergqvist rebuilds the Icehotel from 50,000 tons of snow, designing a fresh new version each winter.

Art

Long before the functional, simple style of contemporary Swedish design, the Vikings adorned weapons, everyday objects, and ceremonial items with finely wrought carvings. Platters, bowls, and cups of iron and copper portray scenes from Viking legends. Grave sites and barrows have yielded a rich array of weapons and armor decorated with intricate interlocking patterns and fierce warriors of mythology. On many rune stones, pictorial carvings add details to the information conveyed by the runes. Expert silversmiths made jewelry and smaller weapons, and applied inlays to larger metal objects.

Carved wooden designs on the first Christian churches of the Vikings show a mixture of pagan and Christian motifs. Centuries after the Vikings disappeared, the tradition of complex woodcarvings continued within Sweden's Catholic Church. Many medieval churches contain ornate interior scrollwork and carved baptismal fonts. In the fifteenth century, the German sculptor Bernt Notke carved the famous statue of Saint

These bold art glass pieces were created by the Swedish designer Helen Kranz, who seeks to imbue her work with a sense of rhythm.

George and the Dragon for Stockholm's Storkyrkan.

The late nineteenth century produced some of Sweden's greatest artists. As the population urbanized and moved away from the countryside, sculptors and painters depicted pastoral traditions and scenes from mythology. Artists from this period worked in a romantic style, ignoring the more modern styles evolving in Europe. Many of these artists' homes have been preserved and are open to the public. Carl Larsson (1853–1919), Sweden's most beloved artist, created idyllic portrayals of rural daily life in his paintings and illustrations. Larsson's beautifully decorated cottage in Dalarna, now known as Carl Larsson-Garden, contains tapestries woven by his wife, Karin, as well as his own work. His close friend, the impressionist painter and sculptor Anders Leonhard Zorn (1860–1920), also lived and worked in Dalarna. The internationally recognized sculptor Carl Milles (1875–1955) created a Poseidon fountain as Göteborg's city centerpiece. During his lifetime, he put together a sculpture

Located at Stockholm's city hall, this statue depicts St. George on horseback slaying a dragon. St. George's deeds of bravery, including the heroic rescue of maidens, date from the early sixth century and are legendary throughout Europe.

Carl Larsson (1853–1919) was one of Sweden's most beloved artists. This watercolor painting is titled *In the Hawthorn Hedge*. Larsson is famous for his depictions of family life in Sundborn, where he lived. Today, nearly 60,000 people visit Larsson's house each year.

garden in his northern Stockholm home, where he displayed pieces from antiquity and the Renaissance as well as his own work.

In the twentieth century, this romantic and classical school gave way to modernism, abstraction, and surrealism. Some artists such as the sculptor and painter Bror Hjorth (1894–1968) turned to his Swedish folk roots for inspiration. Sweden has made a creative mark on the world not through its visual arts, however, but through its sleek and functional design of goods and house wares. This elegant style began with the crafts of individual artisans, mainly in Dalarna, and spread in the early twentieth century to industrial design and manufacturing.

Swedish craftspeople create pottery, baskets, rugs, weavings, and brightly colored national costumes, drawing on traditional techniques and personal artistry.

Carl Milles (1875–1955) created this sculpture, which is on display at the Carl Milles Museum in Stockholm, Sweden. At one time Milles's home, the museum now holds over 160 of his works, many of which are in the garden overlooking the sea.

Anders Leonhard Zorn (1860–1920) was a famous Swedish painter, etcher, and sculptor. Zorn is also known for his portraits, including those of three American presidents.

The wooden, red-painted Dalecarlian horse, Dala for short, has come to stand as one of Sweden's unofficial national symbols. Swedish furniture is often made of light-colored woods, such as blond pine or birch. Little decoration goes into traditional furniture, resulting in simple pieces with smoothly defined lines. The Swedish firm IKEA brought sleek, inexpensive functionality to homes around the world, introducing traditional Swedish designs to an appreciative international audience.

The "Kingdom of Glass" in Smålond is home to many industrial glassblowing firms and small glass artisan studios. Artists and designers produce pieces of all varieties, notable for simple practicality, elegant lines, or creative whimsy. Famous companies such as Orrefors offer both luxury art glass and cut crystal, or more traditional items along classical lines.

To the north, the Samish craftspeople work with materials native to Norrland, such as birch wood, reindeer horn, leather, and bone. Traditional crafts include knives and sheaths, utensils, bowls, jewelry, and vivid embroidery, often decorated in much

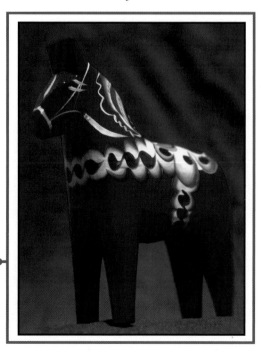

Perhaps one of the best-known symbols of Sweden today, Dalecarlian horses (Dalahäst in Swedish) were first created in the seventeenth century by Swedish woodsmen sitting by firelight in the evening. They became internationally famous when a giant Dalecarlian horse was placed at the entrance to the Swedish pavilion of the 1939 World's Fair. Bob Hope, Elvis Presley, and Bill Clinton have all received Dalecarlian horses.

Swedish glass is world renowned for being beautiful and innovative. Sweden's tradition as a glassmaking country dates to the 1500s when King Gustav Vasa opened a glass-works in Stockholm. Here, contemporary glass masters shape an elegant piece of crystal.

the same style as Viking artifacts. Some Sami still wear traditional garments as everyday clothing.

Swedish museums receive government funding, so they are usually world-class and inexpensive to visit. The National Museum in Stockholm boasts a collection of artwork ranging from the Middle Ages to contemporary. Skansen, the world's first open-air museum, contains nineteenth-century homes and exhibitions portraying the Swedish lifestyles of centuries past. Throughout his life, Prince Eugen (1865–1947) collected works by Nordic artists, including many by Larsson and Zorn. Waldesmarsudde, the home of Sweden's "painting prince" and his collection, is open to the public. Malmö's Form Design Center features temporary exhibits on the latest innovations in Scandinavian architecture and design. The Stockholm Metro— the city's subway—is known as the "world's

Sweden's Skansen Folk Museum, an open-air museum located in Stockholm, was the first of its kind in the world. Visitors are welcomed at each historic site by guides dressed in appropriate period clothing.

longest art exhibition." Most stations are decorated by commissioned works for an ongoing project that began in the 1950s.

Theater and Film

The Swedish government generously funds performing arts programs. It recognizes forms as diverse as puppet and mime theaters and a growing amateur theater community in addition to classical theater productions and renowned institutions such as the Royal Opera. Sweden's Kungliga Dramatiska Teatern—Royal Dramatic Theater—is the most prestigious in the nation. Movie icon Greta Garbo made her debut on this stage during the first half of the twentieth century, and filmmaker Ingmar Bergman (1918–) directs two plays here every year. Sweden's most dynamic theater scene is in Stockholm, but even Swedes in rural areas can take advantage of the performing arts. The Riksteatern, or National Traveling Theater, performs plays all over the country. The Swedish Institute estimates that Swedes make about four million trips to the theater a year.

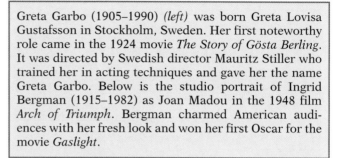

Greta Garbo (1905–1990) *(left)* was born Greta Lovisa Gustafsson in Stockholm, Sweden. Her first noteworthy role came in the 1924 movie *The Story of Gösta Berling*. It was directed by Swedish director Mauritz Stiller who trained her in acting techniques and gave her the name Greta Garbo. Below is the studio portrait of Ingrid Bergman (1915–1982) as Joan Madou in the 1948 film *Arch of Triumph*. Bergman charmed American audiences with her fresh look and won her first Oscar for the movie *Gaslight*.

Early Swedish directors from the days of silent film remain prominent influences to modern filmmakers. Victor Sjöström (1879–1960) caught Europe's attention with his first film, *Ingeborg Holm* (1913), a critical examination of injustice within Sweden's legal system. Mauritz Stiller (1883–1928) captivated audiences with his witty and lighthearted comedies like *Erotikon* (1920), in which a scientist falls in love with a beautiful young woman while his wife has an affair with his best friend.

After the silent era passed, Swedish film lost much of its former cultural relevance in favor of slapstick comedy, though Swedish actresses Greta Garbo and Ingrid Bergman became stars. Filmmaking in Sweden reached an international audience when director Ingmar Bergman emerged in the 1950s. Bergman focused on death, morality, and the hidden human psyche, often touching on spiritual themes. His dark, moody masterpieces, including *The Seventh Seal* and *Through a Glass Darkly*, remain benchmarks for other directors. He was honored for lifetime achievement by the Directors Guild of America in 1990.

Bergman retired from film in the early 1980s to work in theater. A new crop of Swedish directors took over. Of these, Lasse Hallström (1946–) has achieved the most popular success with a pair of

critically acclaimed films. *My Life as a Dog* and *What's Eating Gilbert Grape?* closely examine less-than-ideal family situations in a warm and sympathetic light. Lukas Moodysson's (1969–) films often focus on the interactions of close-knit friends and social groups. *Tillsammans* (2000) joyfully presents a group of socially-conscious Swedes living together in a commune during the mid 1970s. Roy Andersson's (1943–) works like *Sånger Från Andra Våningen* (2000) are more unsettling, commenting on humanity's vulnerability and need for companionship.

Swedish director Ingmar Bergman (right) and cinematographer Sven Nyquist are shown here as they shoot the 1982 film *Fanny och Alexander* (Fanny and Alexander). Born in Uppsala, Sweden, in 1918, Bergman is best known as a prolific filmmaker who writes and directs films dealing with spiritual and psychological conflicts. His first international success came in 1955 with the film *Sommarnattens Leende*, an adaptation of Shakespeare's *A Midsummer Night's Dream*. Bergman has won three Oscars, all for Best Foreign Language Film.

THE LITERATURE AND MUSIC OF SWEDEN

8

Very few remnants of Swedish Viking and medieval literature remain, except for a handful of religious works dating before 1500. Queen Kristina first encouraged the flowering of literature in the 1640s, and Gustav III later brought the fine arts to his court. He established the Swedish Academy of Literature in 1786. Intellectual and scientific principles of the Enlightenment spread to Sweden, influencing the mystical writings of theologian and scientist Emmanuel Swedenborg (1688–1772). The most notable writers of the era were poets, the greatest being Carl Michael Bellman (1740–1795). He lived a colorful life, at one point fleeing to Norway to avoid creditors. His verses, largely biblical in theme, followed the Enlightenment ideals combined with a wry wit and a satirical slant on life's realities. He set most of his works to music and they remain popular today. The botanist and physician Carl von Linné, also known as Carolus Linnaeus, spent most of his life working on the immense *Systema Naturae*. It presents a system of classification including every living organism and earned him the informal title, "father of taxonomy."

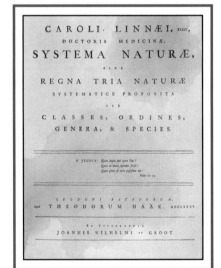

The beginning of the nineteenth century saw the founding of a new dynasty of Swedish rulers. Poetry flowered during the conservative reign of King Karl Johan, taking on a style influenced by German Romanticism. Writers of this genre often chose Swedish nationalistic themes grounded in folk culture.

The portrait on the left is Swedish mystic and scientist Emanuel Swedenborg (1688–1772), who became convinced that he had direct access to the spiritual world after having a series of dreams. The document above is the title page of Carolus Linnaeus's *Systema Naturae*, printed in Leyden in 1735. Linnaeus's book is a culmination of his studies to organize plant and animal forms into one classification system.

This portrait of Swedish poet and musician Carl Michael Bellman (1740–1795) is housed at the Royal Library in Stockholm. Bellman wrote over seventeen hundred poems, most set to music. His work is still popular throughout much of Scandinavia.

When King Karl's son Oscar ushered in a more liberal age upon taking the throne in 1844, the tone of literature abruptly shifted once again. Writers penned realistic novels addressing social issues. In 1879, August Strindberg (1849–1912) published *The Red Room*, a satire on class relations in Stockholm society that caused a sensation in the literary world. His writing rejuvenated Swedish literature and influenced the genre of drama. Psychological drama, a character's alienation from the world, and social themes run through his works. The Swedish Academy and the literary establishment ignored him, but his countrymen recognized him as a master of Swedish literature. The workers' movement raised a large sum of money and awarded him the "Anti-Nobel Prize." A group of young writers known as *Unga Sverige*, or Young Sweden, followed Strindberg's example in attacking Sweden's social and political establishments.

A few of Sweden's prominent authors of this time followed their own personal styles rather than the prevailing trends. Selma Lagerlöf (1858–1940) focused on Swedish legend and rural life. Her first novel, *Gösta Berling's Saga* (1891), tells a swashbuckling story of adventure and romance set in Värmland. Her best-known book is *The Wonderful Adventures of Nils*, a children's tale that brings to life Sweden's land and history.

This portrait of Carolus Linnaeus was painted circa 1760. Linnaeus, a Swedish naturalist, developed the modern scientific systems for naming plants.

August Strindberg (1849–1912)

August Strindberg was Sweden's greatest playwright. He was also a novelist, an artist, a short-story writer, a photographer, and, some say, a madman. Born in Stockholm to a merchant and a former waitress, he would later title his autobiography *The Son of a Servant*. He studied medicine at Uppsala University only to drop out after a single semester. Charles XV eventually financed his continued studies at Uppsala in recognition of one of his early plays, *The Outlaw*, although Strindberg dropped out once again. After returning to Stockholm, he worked as a journalist and a librarian at the Royal Library and married Siri von Essen in 1875. Publication of *The Red Room* and subsequent controversial works brought him both fame and notoriety. In 1882, he and his family left Sweden to travel abroad for six years. He revisited Sweden briefly in 1884 to defend himself in court on a blasphemy charge over his short-story collection, *Married*. Although he was acquitted, the experience affected his already unstable personality. He returned to Stockholm in 1889, a depressed alcoholic, divorced his wife in 1891, and left again to travel. After a mental and emotional crisis and another brief marriage, he experienced a mystic conversion and felt himself reborn as a writer. He returned to Stockholm in 1899, this time permanently. One last marriage, from 1901 to 1904, inspired some of his late works.

Swedish novelist Selma Lagerlöf is shown here picking flowers in her garden in the 1930s. Her work, written in a romantic style, was deeply rooted in Nordic legend and history. She wrote about peasant life and the landscape of northern Sweden, including *Gösta Berling's Saga*, a two-volume book.

She became the first woman to win the Nobel Prize for literature in 1909.

Gunnar Ekelöf (1907–1968) was one of Scandinavia's greatest poets. He wrote modernist poetry influenced by surrealism, mysticism, and a lifelong interest in the Orient. While Ekelöf expressed his inner visions, his contemporary Pär Lagerkvist (1891–1974) addressed philosophical and religious issues in his poems and novels, dealing with Christian themes outside the context of the Swedish Church. His 1950 novel *Barabbas* tells the story of the thief Pontius Pilate spared from crucifixion instead of Christ. Lagerkvist was awarded the Nobel Prize in 1951.

Many Swedish writers after the turn of the century followed Strindberg's lead and concentrated on social issues. They gave a face to the working class, in a tempestuous time when peasants were moving from the farm to the factory. Moa Martinson (1890–1964), a novelist as well as a journalist, wrote about the daily life of working women in rural Sweden. Her husband, Harry Martinson (1904–1978), told of his poverty-stricken childhood in the autobiographical work *Nässlorna blomma* (Flowering nettles, 1935), and received the Nobel Prize in 1974. Vilhelm Moberg (1898–1973) is best known for his *Emigrants* series written from 1949 to 1959. Set at the turn of the century, it describes the journey of a Smålond family who leave their homeland to become pioneers in Minnesota. These books were made into movies in the early 1970s by Jan Troell.

Some of Sweden's best-known works exist purely for the reader's pleasure rather than for their depth or social message. Frans Bengtsson (1894–1954) wrote *Röde Orm* (The long boats), a Viking tale, in an ornate narrative style similar to the old Icelandic sagas. A national bestseller, it helped revive Swedish interest in the Vikings.

Swedish author Astrid Lindgren (1907–2002) wrote her famous tall tale, *Pippi Longstocking*, for her daughter in 1944. The original cover is at right. The book has been translated into sixty languages and adapted for many films. The rambunctious Pippi Longstocking achieved international success, and Lindgren became Sweden's best-known author.

One of the most beloved characters of children's literature came from Sweden. Astrid Lindgren (1907–2002) told her children fanciful tales of Pippi Längstrump, an unconventional, strong-willed girl unlike most of the sweet and well-behaved heroines of earlier children's books. When she finally published some of these stories in 1945, critics protested the example set by the outspoken main character, but kids and families around the world immediately fell in love with Pippi Longstocking. Lindgren is Sweden's best-selling author, and her books have been translated into more than fifty languages. Stockholm even has an Astrid Lindgren fairy-tale house and museum, which includes a train ride where visitors can travel through the landscapes of her fantastic stories.

Music and Dance

Sweden has a long tradition of both folk and classical music. Although these styles have developed along different lines and appeal to different audiences, they overlap and borrow from each other. Queen Kristina brought the violin to Sweden in the seventeenth century; it became one of the mainstays of folk music. Later, nationalist classical composers would borrow folk melodies for their works.

The Swedes value their musical heritage, and have actively worked to keep up their folk tradition. Institutes preserve musical manuscripts dating from the seventeenth and eighteenth centuries, and keep recordings collected as far back as the first few decades of the twentieth century. A revitalization of interest in folk culture occurred during the 1970s. More people started enjoying and performing Swedish folk music, and scholars

began studying and cataloging archived material. Hobbyists try to reconstruct instruments used in the past, or revive lost performance practices.

The fiddle historically played the most important part of the Swedish folk ensemble. Other common instruments include the accordion, the *sackpipa* (bagpipe), the *vevlira* (hurdy-gurdy), and the *nyckelharpa*. This instrument, the "keyed fiddle," dates back to the Middle Ages. It is played with a bow, and the player presses keys to changes notes produced by each string. Songbooks from the eighteenth and nineteenth centuries show that repertory varied little across Sweden, but musical style differed from one region to another.

In days past, the musicians were amateurs who played for the enjoyment of all or to provide music for dancers. Seventeenth-century Swedes danced the minuet or the cadrille, while in the eighteenth century they enjoyed the waltz or the polska, a triple-meter dance native to Poland that Sweden has adopted as one of its basic musical forms. Folk musicians also brought out ceremonial music on occasions such as weddings. Sometimes a soloist or a small group performed a long ballad while an audience listened or joined in on refrains. Other songs were shorter and everyone could sing along.

Herding Music

In a few green pastures of central Sweden, a mournful high-pitched falsetto call rings out. Miles away, cattle recognize the voice of their herding girl and begin to move in her direction. This technique, known as *kulning*, dates from the Middle Ages, and different calls could reach cattle or communicate messages from one person to another across long distances. Different lengths and numbers of notes in the call sometimes varied depending on the location and occasion.

Instruments such as the *lur*, a birch bark trumpet, or a hollowed-out goat horn could also pass messages or frighten away predators. Today few Swedish women work as herding girls, but musicians preserve the tradition. You might hear kulning at folk music festivals, or even in some contemporary classical music.

The 1930s photo on the left shows a young girl playing a traditional Swedish *lur*, a cone-shaped, wind instrument made of birch. The Swedes use the lur to play folk music.

Jojk, a singing style of Samish folk music, is largely improvisational. Placing equal importance on melody and verse, jojk expresses feelings of sorrow, hate, or love.

The Sami call their folksong the *jojk*. It is an improvised style of singing resembling a chant, and the ideas or feelings expressed hold spiritual significance. Drums traditionally accompany the song, although now other instruments sometimes join the singer as well.

The first form of classical music in Sweden was church music for the Catholic Mass. Sweden did not begin to develop its own classical institutions until the eighteenth century. King Gustav III founded the Royal Academy of Music in 1771, and the Royal Opera of Stockholm in 1773. Most composers and musicians came from abroad. Even Carl Michael Bellman borrowed many of the melodies for his poems from folk music or foreign opera.

The 1900s saw a greater output of music by Swedish composers. Franz Berwald (1796–1868), perhaps Sweden's greatest composer, is best known for his symphonies and chamber music. A trio of talented composers emerged toward the turn of the century. The finest works of Wilhelm Peterson-Berger (1867–1942) are his expressive piano pieces and a symphony based on melodies from Lappland. The pianist and conductor Wilhelm Stenhammar (1871–1927) also composed piano and orchestral music with beautiful melodies. Hugo Alfven (1872–1960) wrote the most nationalistic music of the three, and his *Midsommarvaka* and *Swedish Rhapsodies* are among the best known Swedish compositions.

The Götesborgs Operan in Göteborg, Sweden, is known for the hook-shaped sculpture at the front entrance.

Jenny Lind (1820–1887), the Swedish Nightingale, was America's first pop-culture icon. Nearly 7,000 people attended her first American concert on September 11, 1850. This advertisement, which marked the event, is housed at the Royal Library in Stockholm, Sweden.

Ivar Hallstrom (1826–1901) wrote operas based on Swedish mythology, but Sweden is better known for celebrated opera singers. The superstar soprano Jenny Lind (1820–1887) performed around the world and was courted by Hans Christian Anderson. Birgit Nilsson (born in 1918) was one of the greatest dramatic sopranos of her day. Most major cities have an opera venue. Göteborg constructed the grand new Götesborgs Operan in 1994.

Today, Sweden is the world's third largest exporter of music in the world, trailing only the U.S. and Britain. Best known is the 1970s smash group ABBA. Other recent popular Swedish acts have included Ace of Base, Roxette, the Cardigans, and Inner Circle. Sweden holds a number of music festivals throughout the year and free outdoor performances in the summer. The Falun Folk Music Festival has evolved into a prestigious international music event. Music on Lake Siljan in Dalarna, held in July, presents concerts offering music of all types.

Many Swedes still enjoy folk dancing in traditional costume for holidays and festivals. Gustaf III established the Royal Swedish Ballet in 1773, and today it is affiliated with the Royal Opera. People interested in classical ballets and operas can attend performances at the Drottningholms Slottsteater, an eighteenth-century theater adjacent to the royal castle.

The Swedish musical group ABBA is shown here in a 1979 concert. ABBA's career began in 1974 when the group represented Sweden by singing "Waterloo" in the Eurovision song contest.

FAMOUS FOODS AND RECIPES OF SWEDEN

9

Native Swedish cuisine is simple and hearty, and may seem bland to visitors. In recent years, cities have begun to offer more international options, introducing spices absent in traditional Swedish food. Although the potato has only been grown in Sweden since the nineteenth century, the Swedish have adopted it as a staple in many of their dishes. In the past, the seafaring Swedes relied heavily on fish, but today it is too expensive to eat regularly. A typical meal includes a potato dish and meat, accompanied by bread.

Breakfast food is similar to United States fare, and invariably includes black coffee. The Swedish consume more coffee per capita than almost any other country. The Sami prepare it as *Kaffeost*: they add soft goat cheese to coffee and let it steep, spoon out and eat the lumps of cheese, then drink the coffee.

Traditional everyday dishes may include meatballs, sausage, potatoes, cabbage rolls, thick soups, and fish of all varieties. The Swedish serve caviar as a common accompaniment, not a delicacy. *Pytt i panna* is a one-pot meal of fried potatoes, onions, eggs, and diced meat. On Thursdays, Swedes eat pea soup and pork, and pancakes topped by lingonberry preserves for dessert. This tradition dates back to pre-Reformation times, when the Catholic Church required that Church members fast on Fridays. They fell into the habit of eating this filling Thursday meal to stave off hunger pangs on the following day. The Sami eat a lot of reindeer and wild game, including *bidus*, a reindeer stew. Sweden's national drink is *aquivit* or *snaps*, a highly alcoholic beverage similar to vodka.

In Sweden, the Feast of the Annunciation is known as *Våffeldagen*, or waffle day. Swedes celebrate on March 25 by eating waffles, which they top with strawberry or orange-colored cloudberry jam and whipped cream. Above, a young girl rolls dough in order to make *Pepparkakor*, a traditional holiday spice cookie.

Janssons Frestelse

In 1846, the religious zealot Eric Jansson and 1,200 followers emigrated to Illinois and founded the utopian Bishop Hill colony. Jansson's doctrine stressed the importance of leading a life of austere holiness. Legend tells that one day he was served au gratin of potatoes, onions, and anchovies, smothered in cream and baked. Jansson devoured the entire dish! To this day, "Jansson's Temptation" remains a popular meal.

Most Swedes indulge in custards, cookies, fruit tarts, and other treats for dessert. They combine their appreciation for coffee and sweets in popular afternoon coffee parties, or *kafferep*. The hostess provides a variety of baked goods which customarily includes at least seven different types of pastries or breads.

Special Occasions

The most famous creation of Swedish cuisine is the *smörgåsbord*, or "bread and butter table." Many countries use the term interchangeably with "buffet," but in Sweden it is reserved for special occasions, such as the *Julbord*, served on Christmas Eve. A fine smörgåsbord is a matter of national pride. Swedes consider the invitation to a smörgåsbord an honor. Providing a full meal with dozens of choices, it begins with a plate of fish, followed by cold meats and salads, hot dishes, and finally, a plate of fruit, cheese, and pastries. Sweden's longest smörgåsbord stretched for 730 meters—almost half of a mile!

A variety of traditional Swedish cookbooks are shown here. In Sweden, food is generally simple, filling, and healthful.

Pepparkakor
A traditional holiday spice cookie

1/2 cup molasses	1 egg	1/2 teaspoon ginger
1/2 cup packed brown sugar	2 1/2 cups flour	1/2 teaspoon cinnamon
1/2 cup butter	1/4 teaspoon baking soda	1/2 teaspoon cloves

1. In a medium saucepan, cook molasses and brown sugar until just boiling. Add butter and stir until melted. Remove from heat. Beat the egg and stir in.
2. Mix flour, soda, and spices in a medium bowl. Add to wet ingredients and combine well.
3. Pat the dough into a disc and wrap in plastic wrap. Refrigerate for at least two hours.
4. Preheat oven to 350° F. Roll out a quarter of the dough to a thickness of 1/8 inch on a lightly floured surface. Cut out shapes with a cookie cutter and transfer to a greased baking sheet. Bake for six to eight minutes. Repeat with remaining dough.

5. Decorate with icing or sprinkles if desired. Store in an airtight container.

The Swedish have a special food to match almost every festive event. Some holidays receive little notice except for a traditional meal or treat. Annunciation Day, or *Vår Fru Dag*, is better known as Waffle Day. Since Vår Fru is pronounced much like *våffel* (waffle), it provides an excuse to indulge in delicious Swedish waffles! On *Midsommar*, the traditional meal includes a variety of herring dishes, fresh potatoes, and strawberries.

August is the month for outdoor crayfish parties, a delicacy to the Swedes. These small shellfish are usually boiled and served in a dish full of brine, and eaten as finger-food. Northerners might instead throw *Surströmming* parties. Surströmming is Baltic herring fermented for a year until it is half rotted. Swedes eat this odd-smelling specialty rolled in flat bread with boiled potatoes and onions. On November 10, Saint Martin's Day, many still eat a supper of roast goose and soup made from goose blood. The Christmas Eve *Julbord* is a huge meal, including ham, sausages, meatballs, herring, plums, *lutfisk* (dried codfish soaked in lye and then boiled), rice pudding, and a variety of smaller selections.

DAILY LIFE
AND CUSTOMS IN
SWEDEN

10

I t is a beautiful July day in Göteborg, one of Sweden's most dynamic cities. But despite the temperate, sunny weather, few people can be seen enjoying the day. The trams and streets are nearly empty, and some shops and restaurants are closed. Only a handful of children play in parks and yards.

Most people have taken their annual vacation and gone to the country for the month. Ninety percent of the Swedish live in towns and cities, but they still feel a deep connection to nature and the outdoors. There are over 600,000 vacation homes in Sweden, many near the water. Every Swede dreams of owning a country house as well as their home in the city. They escape to the country for weekends and vacations, and love outdoor activities.

Life in a Welfare State

The Swedes have good lives. They earn some of the highest per capita incomes in the world, although sales and income taxes can soar to as much as 25 percent. With the help of this hefty tax revenue, government programs steer a "middle way" between socialism and capitalism, guaranteeing a high quality of life for the population. The poor can receive housing

A mother teaches her child to ski *(left)*. Although popular throughout Europe and America, skiing as a sport is relatively new. However, evidence of a preserved pair of skis from central Sweden shows that skiing as a means of travel dates back to 2500 BC. During wars of the sixteenth and seventeenth century Swedish commanders equipped all their troops with either skis or snowshoes. But it was not until 1924 that cross-country skiing and ski jumping became the first skiing sports events of the Olympic Winter Games. Small, red cottages throughout the countryside *(above)* have become a national symbol for Sweden. This is not so much because the red cottages look so quaint but because the red paint is made from the red ore that comes out of Sweden's Falun copper mine.

This is a vat of the red paint containing copper from the Falun copper mine used to paint Swedish cottages. The copper helps prevent the paint from corroding. The Falun copper mine closed in 1992 except for providing copper for the red paint.

grants and unemployment benefits. Unlike the limited U.S. system, welfare programs enrich the lives of the entire population. All citizens and many noncitizens are eligible for free health and dental care, regardless of income. Swedish public schools provide an excellent education, unions protect jobs and working conditions, and the government funds recreational activities and the arts.

Labor laws help protect jobs—employees cannot be fired except in drastic circumstances. Employers allow a liberal policy on sick days and personal time off, including a minimum paid vacation of five weeks. These standards do not often bring the government in conflict with business, since most companies are worker-friendly.

The average Swedish household consists of two children and their parents. It is common for unmarried couples to live together and have children, and a law called *sambolagen* gives them the same rights as married couples. Sweden has a high divorce rate, so single-parent families, usually headed by the mother, are also typical. On average, women have their first child at the age of twenty-eight, and a pregnant woman takes off a month of paid leave from work before the child is

The staff members of a Swedish magazine publisher in Stockholm are working on computers.

born. Afterward, the parents share fifteen months of paid child-care leave. Children generally enter government subsidized daycare at the age of two before enrolling in school at six years of age.

Parents encourage independence in their children, and most young adults leave home by the age of eighteen. In Sweden, youths are more likely to live alone than with a group of friends, as is common in the United States. Students who study at a university receive generous government aid, and do not need to depend on their parents financially.

Similarly, the elderly hang on to their independence as long as they can. Swedes have exceptionally long life expectancies, and lead active lifestyles even after retirement. The government helps them stay in their own homes as long as possible, providing assistants to occasionally help with household tasks or shopping if necessary. They usually enter a retirement community when they can no longer live at home; very few move in with adult children.

Leisure Time

The Swedes tend to favor a quiet life rather than keep up a busy social network. Most families do not go out for dinner very often, preferring a home-cooked meal, although workers eat lunch at restaurants near their workplaces. The *dagens rätt*, or daily special, is inexpensive and substantial. The Swedes bake bread and prepare

It's fall in Lapland as a family of Swedish hikers cooks a hearty outdoor meal.

On March 3, 2002, 14,000 competitors gathered at the starting line of the annual Vasaloppet ski race in Sälen, Sweden. The skiers crossed 56 miles (90 km) of dense forest to Mora, Sweden, in what many Swedes call a valiantness certificate or test of strength.

food from scratch, including condiments such as salad dressing and jam. Families enjoy putting their love of nature to a practical use and spend time hunting, fishing, and gathering food from public land. Wild berries and edible mushrooms are bountiful during the temperate months.

Table manners are very formal, whether at a family meal or a dinner party. The hosts expect guests to arrive on time, and it is very rude to arrive even a few minutes late. Considerate guests bring a small gift such as flowers or a bottle of wine, and remove their shoes before going inside. The Swedes tend to be reserved and have little use for small talk, shying away from controversial topics such as politics and religion, and dislike discussing business during their leisure time. Safe subjects include the weather or sports. After the meal, everyone says, "Tack för maten" to thank the cook. The next time guests see the host, it is polite to say "Tack för senast," or "one last thanks."

Swedes enjoy shopping, and spend much of their income on food, clothing, and the home. Most frown upon showiness, preferring tasteful and functional home furnishings. Casual clothes are the norm, even for work. People dress up more for social occasions out of respect for their hosts. Goods tend to be of a high quality but

Swedish tennis pro Bjorn Borg kisses the men's singles trophy at the Wimbledon Tennis championships after winning it for the fifth time on July 5, 1980.

Right of Public Access

Swedes love to take advantage of the outdoors. But an important part of their connection to the land lies in their respect for nature's delicate balance. An unofficial "right of public access" governs good manners in the wilderness. These common sense rules bring together the Swedish love

of the land and their environmental conscience.

They may hike, ride bikes or horses, and even camp on private property as long as they do not disturb crops or stray close to residences. It is even okay to cross fenced-in pastureland! They may not drive off-road or jet ski except in specific areas, however. Hunting is forbidden on public land, and they must not harm plants and animals. This rule pertains to cutting brush, gathering eggs, or letting a dog run loose during late spring and summer. Fishing is usually permitted, though in some places a license is required. They can build fires if they follow practical safety measures. They may not light fires on bare rocks, since heat could crack and scar them. Needless to say, people are responsible for their own trash, and must leave any site as pristine as they found it.

expensive. Swedish currency is the *krona* (plural *kronor*), and there are about 10.5 kronor per American dollar. This value has fallen in recent years: compared to 5.7 kronor per dollar thirty years ago. Sweden has not adopted the euro, although the country continues to deliberate about it.

If you ask some Swedes about their favorite pastimes, they will all name a few outdoor diversions. Each town has a government-funded *fritidsnämnden,* or recreation

Swedish Massage

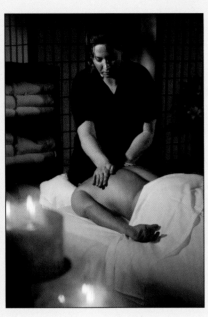

Swedish massage cannot perform magic, but doctors are beginning to marvel at the therapeutic benefits of this favorite means of relaxation. It can reduce stress, promote healing, and help circulation, among many other benefits. The practice dates back to the 1830s, when a man named Per Henrick Ling (1776–1839) wanted to figure out why exercise helped diminish the arthritis in his arm. When he studied in Copenhagen as a young man, he took up gymnastics and fencing. After his return to Sweden, the king approved his proposal to open an athletic institute in the hope that it might bolster Sweden's lackluster military, and the Royal Gymnastics Central Institute opened in 1814. During his long tenure there, Ling developed a system of gymnastics and Swedish massage. His massage techniques and theories stemmed from studies of physiology and travels throughout Europe, Asia, and India researching traditional therapies.

committee, to organize public activities, both outdoors and inside. Sweden boasts thousands of sports clubs aimed at all different lifestyles and athletic interests. The national parks offer many opportunities for visitors. Enthusiasts can camp in between days of mountaineering and rock climbing, or of hiking the thousands of miles of trails that crisscross national land.

Ice fishing is a popular winter sport and family activity in Sweden. To the right, a young boy ice fishes during a Swedish winter.

Although Swedes bemoan the country's long winters, they take full advantage of sports involving snow and ice. Skiing is immensely popular, whether it's cross-country, downhill, or ski jumping. One of the notable events of the season is the world's longest cross-country race, the *Vasaloppet*, stretching for 56 miles (90 kilometers). It re-creates Gustav Vasa's cross-country flight to Norway, which led to a Swedish revolt against the Danish in 1521. Over ten thousand people participate each year, averaging eight hours to complete the course. Swedes also enjoy skating, ice hockey, dog sledding, and ice fishing.

Like most Europeans, the Swedes are avid fans of soccer, and participate in a variety of other sports. Ever since Bjorn Borg became a superstar, tennis has retained a dedicated following. Teens compete annually for the Donald Duck cup, and the Stockholm Open is a prestigious international tournament. The Swedes also participate in horseback riding and races.

With a sweeping coastline, thousands of lakes, rivers, and canals, and a capital city located in an archipelago, the Swedish indulge in every possible water activity. They travel in yachts, kayaks, motorboats, canoes, and sailboats, sometimes equipped for fishing. Many rivers are ideal for rafting. On the waterfront, one can see swimmers, surfers, and sunbathers. Stockholm holds a weeklong Water Festival in August, with festivities and entertainment as well as water-related activities and information.

Winter forces the Swedes indoors for much of the year, and they have found many interests to preserve them through the long, cold nights. They read voraciously, gobbling up newspapers, magazines, and more books per capita than any other European nation. A high-tech nation, Sweden is well wired, with an Internet-savvy population. Most households have a television set. Swedes love music, and over 600,000 people of all ages sing in choral groups.

EDUCATION AND WORK IN SWEDEN

11

Alarm clocks ring early across the household. The family meets briefly for a *"God morgon!"* ("Good morning!") and grabs a quick breakfast. Then family members each go their separate ways for the day. Most parents work, while children attend child care or school. After completing twelve years of public school, a majority of students graduate equipped with specialized professional skills and immediately enter a highly skilled labor force.

Education

Swedish children are required to attend nine years of school, beginning at age six or seven, but many enroll in daycare or preschool programs at an earlier age. The government provides quality child care in order to allow parents to work or pursue further education without needing to worry about the well-being of their children. Swedes consider early childhood education crucial to a person's later development.

Daycare programs aim to keep children content and pique their interest through games, educational activities, and group work. Kindergarten is not mandatory, although most children attend preschool, or *forskoleklass*, which prepares them for later schooling and encourages cooperation with others. The Swedes believe in allowing youngsters plenty of playtime, both in preschool and early compulsory school.

The woman *(left)* reads to children at a Swedish daycare center in Stockholm. Sweden's child care system has two goals: to make it possible for parents to combine parenting and employment, and to support and promote the development of children. The photograph above was taken in the emergency room at Astrid Lindgren Youth Hospital.

These are Swedish textbooks. In addition to core studies mandated by the Swedish government, high school students, during their upper secondary education years, must elect a special course of study from sixteen choices.

Over 96 percent of Swedish children receive government-funded public education, but a few choose private schools for religious or personal reasons. Home schooling is not allowed. Whenever possible, parents may choose which public school their children attend. The school year does not differ much from that of the U.S., lasting for 178 to 190 days with school days six- to eight-hours long. School stays in session from mid-August to early June, allowing a Christmas vacation, a one-week "sports holiday" in February, and an Easter break.

Students receive free books, school supplies, and hot lunches. During their first three years of school, they begin to learn English. Other subjects include Swedish, math, the natural sciences, technology, social sciences, arts, music, and physical education. The curriculum places a greater emphasis than U.S. schools on international culture such as world religions. Both boys and girls take courses in home economics, textiles, woodworking, and metalworking. Later in their schooling, most students begin to learn a third language, often French or German. Teachers only begin to assign grades on subjects in the eighth grade: Pass, Pass with Distinction, or Pass with Exceptional Distinction.

The Swedish school system tries to accommodate the diverse needs of the children. If a Samish family wants its children to receive an education in keeping with its own traditions and language, it may choose one of six Sami national schools for grades one to six rather than its regular school. Non-Swedish speakers can take Swedish language classes in combination with some regular school until they are fluent in Swedish. Children with disabilities attend regular schools if possible, or are placed in special education classes. The government also runs leisure time centers called *fritids*. If both parents work, children can study, receive tutoring, and pursue hobbies at a fritid after school or on holidays.

Every Swedish citizen attends school until age sixteen. After that, 98 percent choose to continue their education at upper secondary school, or *gymnasieskolan*, for three years. Students may choose from among fourteen vocational and three academic programs, or follow a self-designed course. In a vocational program, the student spends 15 percent of school hours training at the workplace and will possess the skills to enter the workforce after graduating. A few examples of the vocational courses include business, car mechanics, hotel work, health care, and handicrafts.

Academic programs prepare students for university study, focusing on natural sciences, social sciences, or technology. The learning level of academic studies is equivalent to U.S. college coursework. The gymnasieskolan aims to give young adults a well-rounded education regardless of their programs. Everyone takes classes in core subjects such as art, Swedish, science, math, and English.

Until recently, all men spent about a year in the military soon after completing upper secondary school, serving a term in the Swedish Army, Royal Swedish Navy, or Swedish Air Force. The government has relaxed this requirement slightly since reducing its military size at the end of the Cold War. Although Swedish forces have not fought in a war for hundreds of years, troops serve in peacekeeping missions for the United Nations.

Slightly over 30 percent of gymnasieskolan graduates attend an institution of higher learning soon after their secondary

This is a fifth grade classroom in Sweden. Educational reforms in the 1940s established a nine-year compulsory, comprehensive school program for children. There are specially designed schools for children with disabilities.

schooling. Public institutions run by the government include eleven universities, twenty smaller university colleges, and a number of specialized colleges devoted to subjects such as arts, science, or medicine. Uppsala University, established in 1477, is the most renowned institution in Sweden. The university library keeps a copy of every book published in Sweden as well as many rare manuscripts.

Admission to most colleges and universities is very competitive due to limited available spaces. The number of people choosing higher education has been increasing in the past decade. Students finish their studies in two to five years, depending on their field. Higher education is nearly free, since the government gives each student a study grant as well as a loan to cover living expenses. Each student is required to join the student union, which manages recreational programs and some aspects of student life.

Many Swedes take advantage of adult education, often through correspondence courses or part-time schooling. Subjects can include everything from crafts and car maintenance to computer programming and folk music. Adults who want to expand on their formal schooling may attend a folk school, which can accommodate all levels of learning from basic to preparation for a university. Mainly nonprofit and privately run, these programs offer a variety of programs that can greatly benefit disadvantaged groups, such as immigrants and the disabled. Many are boarding schools that emphasize community and cooperative learning. The goal of these programs is to reduce the educational gap among Sweden's people.

Although Sweden maintains a strict policy of neutrality, the country still supports a military. The Swedish sailors shown here are on the deck of the HMS *Stromstad*, a high-speed missile attack boat.

Work

During the twentieth century, Sweden developed from a poor agrarian society into a high-tech industrial giant. Today, a quarter of the workforce is directly employed in industry, while the majority works in the service sector, often in jobs related to industrial output. Less than 2 percent still pursue agriculture.

Natural resources helped fuel Sweden's early industrial development. Forestry and iron production still contribute significantly to the economy, employing over 100,000 workers. Immense forests provide trees for paper products, pulp, and some timber. Reforestation after logging guarantees that woodlands will not be depleted. Iron ore deposits provide raw materials for industry as well as some iron and steel for export. Rivers offer sites for factories as well as hydroelectric power.

Saab and Volvo lead in one of Sweden's major industries, transportation equipment. Although best known for automobiles, these companies also make trains and

The Education of Crown Princess Victoria

She's a modern-day princess who lives in a seventeenth-century palace. Born in 1977, Princess Victoria began just as any other young girl who likes skiing and horseback riding: preschool, basic school, and an academic upper secondary program focusing on natural and social sciences. But since graduating in 1996, her activities  would impress even the busiest Ivy League student. She has worked with the Royal Households Collection and the Museum of National Antiquities in Stockholm, attended school in France, and studied the procedures of the Swedish government. From 1998 until 2000, she took courses at Yale while completing internships at the United Nations in New York and the Swedish Embassy in Washington, D.C. Since returning to Sweden, she has continued to train with the government, and followed Swedish involvement in the European Union.

The Swedish-American inventor John Ericsson (1803–1889), portrayed here in a black-and-white steel engraving, established the principles of solar energy. He also invented the ship propeller, which he incorporated into his design for the first ironclad warship, the *Monitor*. Commissioned by the Union, the *Monitor* defeated the *Merrimac* in the American Civil War.

airplanes. Electrolux, the company that marketed the first home vacuum cleaner, still manufactures household appliances of all types. Hasselblad produces high-quality cameras and photographic equipment. A Swedish family might display prized Orrefors glasswork on a shelf purchased at IKEA, the store that popularized simple, practical Swedish design.

Two pharmaceutical companies, AstraZeneca and Pharmacia & Upjohn, dominate the industry in Sweden and play a large role in the world market. Swedish corporations recognized the potential for telecommunications and Internet technology in the early days of the technological boom. The largest, Ericsson, which started manufacturing telephones in 1878, has since kept up with the times, and today produces many of the world's cellular phones.

A recession during the early 1990s forced changes in the government's economic policy as well as affected industry and Swedish workers. Many companies merged to form large international corporations or moved out of Sweden. Ford now owns the Volvo car corporation, and IKEA's headquarters are located in Holland.

About 70 percent of Swedes work in the service sector, in banks, hospitals, retail stores, restaurants and hotels, education, and many other trades. Over a third of these jobs belong to the public sector rather than private interests, since the government owns most schools and

This statue of a miner, erected in 1988 and sculpted by Helge Zandén, is located outside of the Falun copper mine in Sweden.

Made in Sweden

Swedish scientists and inventors have given an eclectic range of contributions to the world.

Anders Celsius (1704–1744) developed the Celsius temperature scale.

Carl von Linné (1707–1778), known as Carolus Linnaeus in English, established system of scientific taxonomy.

Gustaf Erik Pasch (1788–1862) patented the safety match.

John Ericsson (1803–1899) invented the propeller and constructed the American Civil War ship the *Monitor*.

Anders Jonas Ångström (1814–1874) established the foundation for the physics field of spectral analysis.

Alfred Nobel (1833–1896) invented and produced vast quantities of dynamite, later instituting the Nobel Prizes as part of his legacy and desire to promote peace.

Lars Magnus Johansson (1864–1943) created the monkey wrench.

Sven Wingquist (1876–1953) invented the spherical ball bearing.

Victor Hasselblad (1906–1978) developed a precision single-lens reflex camera, which American astronauts used to photograph the moon.

Erik Wallenberg (1915–1999) created the Tetra Pak company, which packages liquids such as juice and milk.

Victor Hasselblad

hospitals as well as a number of companies. Many occupations are related to industry, such as transportation, temporary work agencies, and consulting firms.

Relations between management and workers are usually amicable in the Swedish workplace, whether at a large corporation or small business. The company hierarchy is less rigid than in the U.S., and emphasizes teamwork and creativity. Managers interact informally with employees who tend to take initiative in problem solving and decision making. Major decisions are often reached through consensus at all levels rather than by a small management board. The Swedes are quiet and cautious in business just as they are in their personal dealings, so the workplace often has a casual, low-stress atmosphere.

Trade unions have a long history in Sweden, dating back to the second half of the nineteenth century. Four out of five workers belong to one of three trade unions, comprised of blue collar, clerical, and professional workers. In the past, collective bargaining between unions and employers has resulted in most of Sweden's labor legislation, covering job security, workplace safety, and equal rights for women and minorities. Recently, the influence of unions and traditional

This is the cover of the 2003 IKEA catalog. IKEA, the Swedish company of affordable home furnishings, celebrated its fiftieth anniversary in November 2002. Ingvar Kamprad, head of IKEA, divided a day's gross sales of 152 stores in 28 countries, about $60 million dollars, among employees. Regardless of position, each employee received a $2,800 bonus.

cooperation between union leaders and management took a blow during the recession.

The Equal Opportunities Act grants equal rights for women in the workplace, and prohibits discrimination in pay or conduct. More women earn degrees in higher education than men, and almost half of government figures are women. However, women earn slightly less than men and are more likely to hold part-time jobs. Only a few women hold powerful positions such as CEO of a company. Legislation and government programs, such as child care and generous maternity or paternity leave, seek to help parents balance family and careers.

Sweden's workers now hope for a period of prosperity after successfully dealing with the recession of the 1990s. The new Öresund Link provides a bridge to Denmark and a symbolic link to the rest of Europe. For the first time, outside forces will greatly influence Sweden's workforce and way of life. As the population ages, immigrant workers begin to play a more significant role in a largely homogenous culture. Sweden has no effective social policy to integrate an influx of newcomers into Swedish society.

Globalization and membership in the European Union will affect government policies, and possibly even have an impact on Sweden's much prided neutrality. A country long associated with the "middle way" may soon have to reassess its identity.

> Gustaf Erik Pasch, a professor in chemistry, invented the "safety match" in 1844. By 1876, there were 38 safety match factories in Sweden. Over the years, there have been 121 different Swedish match factories. Solstickan, the match company shown here, allocates 10 percent of its sales to the Solstickan Foundation. Established in 1936, the Solstickan Foundation provides assistance for disabled and chronically ill children and elderly adults. Swedish artist Einar Nerman created the design of the Solstickan Boy for these matchbooks.

SWEDEN
AT A GLANCE

HISTORY

Sweden officially became its own nation in 1523. Gustav Vasa claimed the crown and declared Swedish independence. Before Vasa's bold move, Sweden had spent centuries entangled in civil wars and messy international alliances.

Leaders first attempted to create a unified kingdom from the many independent Swedish Viking settlements during the eleventh century. Civil wars between two factions competing for the crown, the Sverkers and the Eriks, divided the kingdom. No single ruler controlled Sweden until Birger Jarl took the throne as a regent in 1248. He founded Stockholm and established the Folkung dynasty. His son Magnus followed him in 1275, setting up a Council of the Realm made up of powerful Swedish leaders to help maintain order. This governing body evolved into the Riksdag.

The Folkung dynasty ended in 1397, following a series of bloody disputes. Sweden became part of the Kalmar Union, united under the same crown as Norway and Denmark. Bitterness toward the other two nations led Sweden to break from the union, beginning a series of wars with both countries. Gustav Vasa and his army ended the cycle by defeating Denmark's King Christian II and declaring Swedish independence in 1523. Vasa's rule ushered in a golden age. His policies brought money and peace to a battered and poor country. His heirs fought to expand Sweden's borders. By the end of the Thirty Years' War in 1658, Sweden dominated the Baltic Sea and was a major world power.

Sweden lost most of its conquered territory in the Great Northern War, fighting against Poland, Russia, and Denmark from 1700 to 1721. By the end, Sweden controlled only Finland, which slipped away to Russia in 1809 after the Napoleonic Wars. King Gustav IV Adolf, the last Vasa monarch, was deposed in favor of one of Napoleon's marshals. Jean-Baptiste Bernadotte took the crown under the name Karl Johan. He took control of Norway, the last military action ever taken by Sweden.

Afterward, Sweden began a policy of international neutrality that remains in effect today. When Norway voted to break away in 1905, the Swedish Riksdag made no objection. Though officially neutral, many Swedes fought against the Red armies during the 1917 Russian revolution and voluntarily joined Finland in its 1939 Winter War with Russia. Sweden did not participate in the First World War, and attempted to remain neutral during World War II. When the Nazi army used the Swedish countryside as a route from Norway to Finland, outraged Allied forces made Sweden end the policy in 1943. More recently, Swedish military personnel have volunteered as United Nations peacekeepers in Africa, the Middle East, and the former Yugoslavia. Sweden leads the world in environmental protection and aid to impoverished nations

ECONOMY

Sweden's Industrial Revolution began in the 1870s, later than in most other developing European countries. The transformation of its citizens from farmers to factory workers occurred quickly, and Sweden has relied on industry for most of the twentieth century. A thriving economy provided for the welfare state. Under this arrangement, the government supported a capitalist system with generous welfare benefits. Sweden, with its limited domestic market, depended on international markets for a large part of its Gross Domestic Product (GDP). Industry benefited from vast natural resources of timber, iron ore, and hydroelectric power. Today, shipyards and mines have given way to production of automobiles, wood pulp, electrical and telecommunications equipment, and chemicals.

Swedish companies have become pioneers of the pharmaceutical and biotech industries. Ninety percent of industry is privately owned. Agriculture only employs two percent of the workforce; most people work in the service sector.

In the 1990s, Sweden fell into the most severe recession since the depression of the 1930s. Swedish goods slipped on the international market, and many companies merged with rivals or moved out of the country. Unemployment soared, reaching levels as high as 14 percent. The value of the *krona* dropped. Government leadership changed hands, and politicians implemented cutbacks to the extensive welfare system. In 1995, voters narrowly chose to join the European Union.

Government intervention helped Sweden make an economic comeback. The *krona* stabilized and unemployment has dropped to 4 percent. Inflation remains low. The GDP is once again on an upswing. Still, the country may face drastic changes in the next decade. Corporations confront new challenges on the world markets, and will have to work with the government to build future successes. The recession caused a widening gap between the rich and the poor, a new phenomenon among the traditionally egalitarian Swedes.

The number of retirees is increasing and more immigrants are entering the workforce. A contentious issue is the proposed decommission of Sweden's twelve nuclear reactors, a plan opposed by businesses concerned about a possible energy crisis. Involvement with the European Union will require Sweden to reconsider many positions fundamental to current policies. Some economic deregulation and other structural reforms have already been passed in order to gain eligibility to the EU. Many Swedes worry that conforming to the EU's standards will weaken some of Sweden's more progressive policies, such as environmental measures and minority labor laws. Businesses and the government hope that membership will bring an economic resurgence. Swedes rejected adoption of the euro currency in 1997, and will revisit the issue in 2003.

Today, Sweden's per capita GDP is $22,200 per household, the twenty-third highest in the world. (Per capita GDP for the U.S. is $36,200.) The Swedes have a high standard of living and excellent working conditions. The welfare system remains one of the most extensive in the world, despite recent cutbacks.

A skilled and well-educated workforce helped the economy recover after the 1990s recession. Sweden has no minimum wage. Eighty-seven percent of workers belong to unions, which promote labor legislation.

GOVERNMENT AND POLITICS

A 1974 constitution dictates the structure and procedures of the Swedish government. King Karl XVI Gustaf is the nominal head of state. Wielding no political power, he performs only ceremonial and symbolic governmental duties. Crown Princess Victoria will become the next Swedish monarch.

The Riksdag, or parliament, constitutes the legislative branch. The Riksdag, a governmental body distantly descended from the Viking organization known as the *thing*, is a unicameral house of 349 members chaired by the speaker. Many issues are discussed in committees, which formulate proposals to put before the entire *Riksdag*. Swedish residents over eighteen may vote in parliamentary elections, held every four years.

The current parliament, elected in 1998, includes seven political parties. Five of these, the Social Democrats, Conservatives, Leftists, Centrists, and the Liberals, have dominated politics since the 1930s. The Green Party and the Christian Party emerged recently in response to specific issues. The Social Democrats (41.3 percent of current Riksdag members) have been the majority party almost continuously since 1936. Minority parties include the Conservatives (15.8 percent), largely of the business and professional sector, the Liberal Party (13.8 percent), the Christian Democrats (9.5 percent), and the Green Party (4.9 percent), also known as the Ecology Party. Women now hold 43 percent of the parliamentary seats.

The Riksdag elects a prime minister, who serves as head of the government, the executive branch of the Swedish state. This official appoints a cabinet and ministers to direct administrative decisions and implementation. Government ministries draft bills to present to the *Riksdag* and manage international relations. A Riksdag committee checks that government activities comply with the law and the constitution. The position of prime minister does not have term limits, since the Riksdag can nominate a prospective replacement at any time. Göran Persson, a Social Democrat, was elected prime minister in 2002.

The prime minister and the cabinet appoint judges to the five-member supreme court. They rule on cases that have passed through the district courts and the courts of appeal. The parliamentary ombudsman, chosen by the Riksdag, handles complaints against public servants and examines the fair implementation of laws. Every year the ombudsman presents a report to the Riksdag.

Two Swedish ministers are well remembered by the world. Dag Hammarskjöld served as the United Nations secretary from 1953 until his death in 1961, when his plane crashed on a trip to Africa. He was posthumously awarded the Nobel Peace Prize. In 1986, the popular Prime Minister Olof Palme was shot and killed by an unknown assassin. The crime, still unsolved, shocked the peace-loving nation.

TIMELINE

10,000 BC

People first migrate to Sweden.

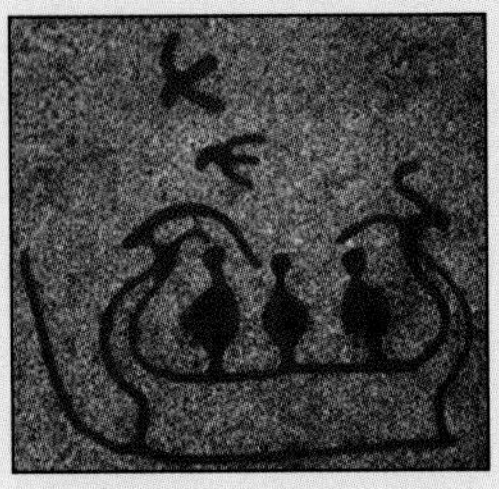

750 BC

Vikings begin exploring.

829

Saint Ansgar introduces Christianity to Sweden.

1060

Olaf Skottkonung destroys the pagan temple at Uppsala.

1814

Sweden gains possession of Norway.

1809

Sweden loses Finland to Russia in the Napoleonic Wars. King Gustav IV Adolf is deposed and a new constitution enacted, dividing power between the monarchy and the Riksdag.

1832

The Göta Canal opens.

1842

Compulsory schooling is instituted.

1921

Universal suffrage granted to all Swedes over twenty-four.

1939-1945

Sweden remains neutral through World War II.

1973

Carl XVI Gustav becomes king.

1974

Constitution revised to current form.

1980

Act of Succession gives women the right to ascend the throne.

1347
Union of Kalmer unites Sweden, Norway, Finland, and Denmark.

1523
Gustav Vasa declares Swedish independence.

1648
The Thirty Years War ends, leaving Sweden one of Europe's greatest powers.

1721-1772
Sweden's "Era of Liberty"

1864-1866
Constitutional revisions limit the monarch's power.

1887
Social Democratic Party emerges.

1905
Norway ends its union with Sweden.

1914-1918
Sweden remains neutral through World War I.

1901
The first Nobel Prize is awarded.

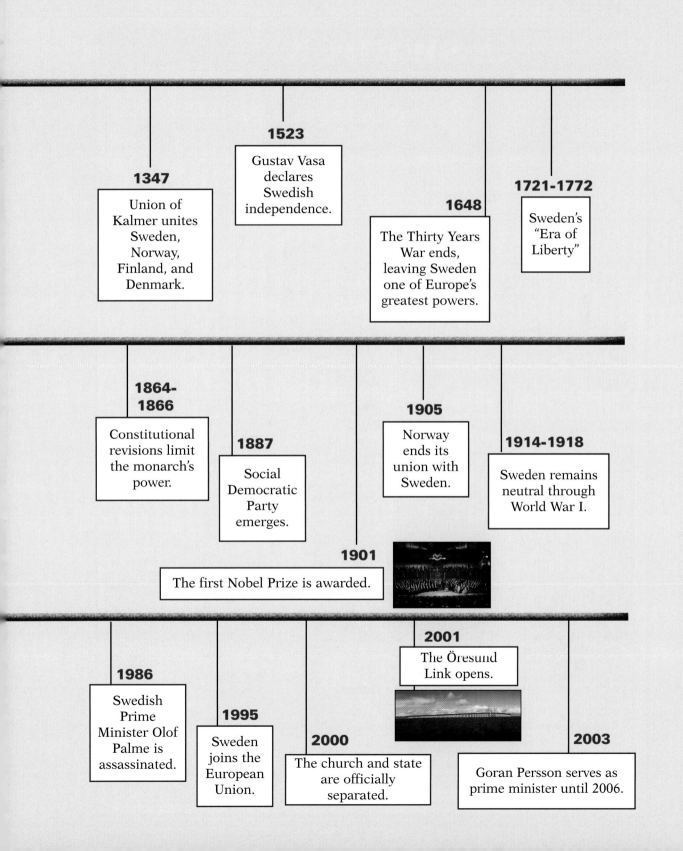

1986
Swedish Prime Minister Olof Palme is assassinated.

1995
Sweden joins the European Union.

2000
The church and state are officially separated.

2001
The Öresund Link opens.

2003
Goran Persson serves as prime minister until 2006.

SWEDEN

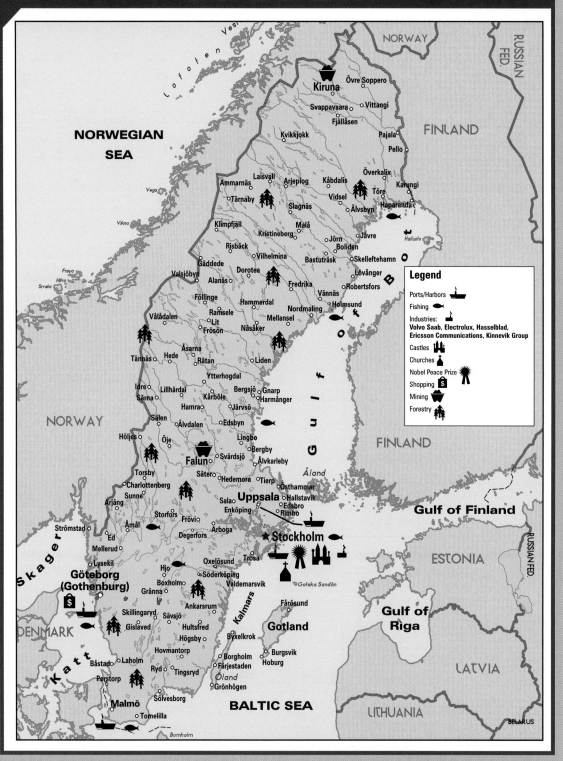

NORWAY

RUSSIAN FED.

Övre Soppero

Kiruna

Svappavaara · Vittangi

Fjällåsen

FINLAND

Kvikkjokk

Pajala

Pello

Laisvall · Arjeplog · Kåbdalis · Överkalix

Ammarnäs · Vidsel · Töre · Karungi

Tärnaby · Slagnäs · Älvsbyn · Haparanda

Klimpfjäll · Malå

Kristineberg · Jörn

Risbäck · Vilhelmina · Boliden

Gäddede · Dorotea · Bastuträsk · Skellefehamn

Valsjöbyn · Alanäs · Fredrika · Lövånger

Föllinge · Vännäs · Robertsfors

Vålådalen · Ramsele · Hammerdal · Holmsund

Lit · Mellansel · Nordmaling

Tännäs · Hede · Fröson · Nåsåker

Åsarna · Rätan · Liden

Ytterhogdal

Idre · Lillhärdal · Bergsjö · Gnarp

Särna · Kårböle · Harmånger

Hamra · Järvsö

Sälen · Älvdalen · Edsbyn

Höljes · Öje · Lingbo

Falun · Bergby

Svärdsjö · Älvkarleby

Torsby · Säter · Hedemora · Tierp · Åland

Charlottenberg · Östhammar

Sunne · Salao · **Uppsala** · Hallstavik

Arjäng · Enköping · Edsbro · Rimbo

Storfors · Frövio

Strömstad · Arboga

Ed · Degerfors · ★ **Stockholm**

Mellerud · Oxelösund · Trosa

Lysekil · Hjo · Söderköping

Göteborg (Gothenburg) · Boxholm · Valdemarsvik · Gotska Sandön

Gränna · Ankarsrum · Fårösund

Skillingaryd · Sävsjö · **Gotland**

Gislaved · Hultsfred · Byxelkrok

Högsby · Borgholm · Burgsvik

Hovmantorp · Hoburg

Laholm · Ryd · Tingsryd · Färjestaden

Båstad · Öland · Grönhögen

Perstorp

Malmö · Sölvesborg

Tomelilla · **BALTIC SEA**

NORWEGIAN SEA

Lofoten Vest

Vega

Vikna

Freya · Hitra

Smela

NORWAY

Skager

Katt

DENMARK

Bornholm

Gulf of B O

FINLAND

Hailuoto

Åland

ESTONIA · RUSSIAN FED.

Gulf of Finland

Gulf of Riga

LATVIA

LITHUANIA

BELARUS

Legend

Ports/Harbors

Fishing

Industries:
Volvo Saab, Electrolux, Hasselblad, Ericsson Communications, Kinnevik Group

Castles

Churches

Nobel Peace Prize

Shopping

Mining

Forestry

ECONOMIC FACT SHEET

Gross Domestic Product: $197 billion

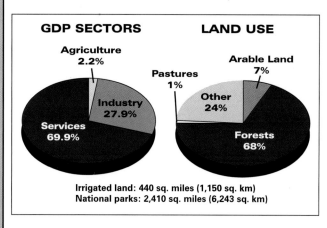

GDP SECTORS

- Agriculture 2.2%
- Industry 27.9%
- Services 69.9%

LAND USE

- Pastures 1%
- Arable Land 7%
- Other 24%
- Forests 68%

Irrigated land: 440 sq. miles (1,150 sq. km)
National parks: 2,410 sq. miles (6,243 sq. km)

Currency and its current U.S. equivalent:
1 krona (Kr) = 100 öre.

Notes: 1, 5, 10, 20, 50, 100, 500, and 1,000 kronor.

Coins: 50 öre; 1, 2, 5, and 10 kronor
$1 = 10.5 Kr

Work Force: 4.4 million

    Agriculture: 2%

    Industry: 24%

    Services: 74%

Major Agricultural Products: Dairy products, grains, sugar beets, potatoes, wood

Major Exports: Wood and paper products, minerals, chemicals and rubber products, machinery and transport equipment, foodstuffs, furniture

Major Imports: Energy, machinery, petroleum and petroleum products, chemicals, motor vehicles, iron and steel, foodstuffs, clothing

Significant Trading Partners:

Export: Germany, United States, Norway, United Kingdom, Denmark

Import: Germany, Norway, Denmark, United Kingdom, Netherlands

Rate of Unemployment: 4%

Highways: 130,960 miles (210,760 kilometers)

Railroads: 7,970 miles (12,820 kilometers)

Waterways: 1,270 miles (2,050 kilometers)

POLITICAL FACT SHEET

Official Country Name:
Konungariket Sverige
(Kingdom of Sweden)

Official Flag: A horizontal
yellow cross on an ocean-blue
field. The motif dates from
the Middle Ages. It was
officially recognized in 1663.

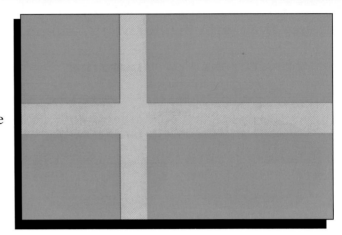

System of Government:
Constitutional monarchy

National Anthem:

"Du gamla, Du fria, Du fjällhöga Nord"
("Thou ancient, thou freeborn, thou mountainous North")
Thou ancient, thou freeborn, thou mountainous North,
In beauty, in peace our hearts beguiling,
I grant thee, thou loveliest land on the earth,
Thy sun, thy skies, thy verdant meadows smiling.
Thy sun, thy skies, thy verdant meadows smiling.

Thy throne rests on mem'ries from great days of yore,
When worldwide renown was valour's guerdon.
I know to thy name thou art true as before.
Oh, I would live and I would die in Sweden,
Oh, I would live and I would die in Sweden.

Federal Structure: The unicameral Riksdag (Parliament) of 349 members acts as
legislative authority. Executive power rests with the prime minister and his fifteen-
to twenty-member cabinet. The judicial branch includes local courts, six superior
courts, and a supreme court. Sweden's monarch holds no political influence.

Number of registered voters: 6,722,152 (1998 parliamentary election)

CULTURAL FACT SHEET

Official Language: Svenska (Swedish)

Major Religions: Lutheran (87%), Catholic, Orthodox, Baptist, Jewish

Capital: Stockholm

Population: 8,913,000

Ethnic Groups: Swedes; Finnish and Samish minorities; foreign-born or first-generation immigrants: Finns, Yugoslavs, Danes, Norweigans, Greeks, Turks

Life Expectancy at birth: male—77.07 years; female—82.5 years

Time: Greenwich Mean Time plus one hour (GMT + 0100)

Literacy Rate: virtually 100%

National Flower: Linnea flower

Cultural Leaders

Visual Arts—Carl Milles, Anders Zorn, Carl Larsson

Literature—August Strindberg, Astrid Lindgrin, Pär Lagerkvist, Selma Lagerlöf

Music—Roxette, ABBA, the Cardigans, Jenny Lind

Entertainment—Lasse Hallstrom, Ingmar Bergman, Greta Garbo, Ingrid Bergman

Sports—Björn Borg

National Holidays and Festivals

Public holidays

New Year's Day—January 1

Epiphany—January 6

Good Friday and Easter—March/April

Labor Day—May 1

Ascension Day—May/June

Whit Monday—late May or early June

Midsummer's Day—
   Saturday nearest June 24

All Saints' Day—November 5

Christmas—December 25

Boxing Day—December 26

Cultural and national celebrations

Walpurgis Night—April 30

Flag Day—June 6

Santa Lucia Day—December 13

Working life

Thirty-five to forty hours per week,
   typically 9 am to 5 pm

Minimum of twenty-five paid vacation days
   as well as twelve public holidays

GLOSSARY

archipelago (ar-kih-PEH-lah-goh) A group of islands.

bicameral (by-KAM-er-ul) A government that has two legislative branches.

biome (BY-ohm) A major type of ecological habitat.

congregation (kahn-gruh-GAY-shun) An assembly of people who routinely meet for religious worship.

coniferous/deciduous (kah-NIH-fur-uhs) / (deh-SID-joo-us) Coniferous trees and shrubs are evergreens and bear cones. The leaves of deciduous trees and plants fall off in autumn.

constitutional monarchy (kon-stih-TOO-shuhn-ul MAH-nar-kee) A government ruled by a constitutional mandate and headed by a largely symbolic monarch.

constitution (kon-stih-TOO-shun) The basic law of a governing body.

dynasty (DY-nah-stee) A successive line of rulers from the same powerful family.

European Union (yur-oh-PEE-an YOON-yun) A cooperative coalition designed to further the interests of European nations.

Gross Domestic Product (GROHS duh-MESS-tik PRA-dukt) A nation's total income, its GDP, as generated by the sum of its economic sectors.

incantation (in-kan-TAY-shun) The spoken part of a magical ritual.

Labor Union (LAY-ber YOON-yun) An organization of workers established to advance its members' interests.

monastery (MAH-nuh-steh-ree) A residence for people under religious vows.

nomad (NOH-mad) A member of a group that has no fixed residence, preferring to move from place to place.

pagan (PAY-guhn) One who belongs to a religion with multiple deities, or does not belong to an organized religion at all.

pantheon (pan-THEE-on) The gods of a people.

polytheistic (pah-lee-thee-IH-stik) Any religion that worships more than one god.

prime minister (PRY-m MIH-nih-ster) The chief executive of a parliamentary state.

tundra (TUN-druh) Treeless plains found in arctic and sub-arctic regions.

unicameral (yoo-nih-KAM-er-uhl) A government body that has a single legislative house.

zealot (ZEL-ot) A fanatical person.

FOR MORE INFORMATION

American Swedish Historical Museum
1900 Pattison Ave
Philadelphia, PA 19145
(215) 389-1776
Web site: http://www.americanswedish.org

American Swedish Institute (Minneapolis)
2600 Park Avenue
Minneapolis, MN 55407

(612) 871-4907
Web site: http://www.americanswedishinst.org

Canadian Nordic Society
PO Box 64126 RPO Holland Cross
Ottawa ON K1Y 4V1
Canada
Web site: http://www.canadiannordicsociety.com

Consulate General of Sweden
One Dag Hammarskjöld Plaza
885 Second Avenue, 45th floor
New York, N.Y. 10017-2201
(212) 583-2550
Web site: http://www.webcom.com/sis/
Consulate of Sweden (Calgary)
1039 Durham Avenue S.W.
Calgary, AB T2T 0P8
(403) 541-0354

Swedish American Museum Center
5211 N Clark St
Chicago, IL 60640
(773) 728-8111
Web site: http://www.samac.org

Swedish Embassy
1501 M Street, NW Suite 900
Washington, DC 20005
(202) 467-2600
Web site: http://www.swedish-embassy.org

Swedish embassy
77 Dalhousie Street
Ottawa, ON K1N 9N8
Canada

(613) 241 8553
Web site: http://www.swedishembassy.ca

Swenson Swedish Immigration Research
    Center
639 38th Street
Rock Island, IL 61201
(309) 794-7204
Web site: http://www.augustana.edu/
    administration/SWENSON/index.htm

United States Tourist Office
655 Third Avenue,
New York, New York 10017-5617
(212) 885-9700
Web site: http://www.gosweden.org

Web Sites

Due to the changing nature of Internet links,
the Rosen Publishing Group, Inc., has
developed an online list of Web sites related to
the subject of this book. This site is updated
regularly. Please use this link to access the list:

http://www.rosenlinks.com/pswc/swed/

FOR FURTHER READING

Branston, Brian. *Gods and Heroes from the Viking Mythology*. New York: Peter Bedrick Books, 1994.

Lagerlof, Selma. *The Wonderful Adventures of Nils*. Mineola, NY: Dover Publications, 1995.

Lindgren, Astrid. *Pippi Longstocking*. New York: Viking Childrens Books, 1997.

Margeson, Susan M. *Eyewitness Books: Viking*. New York: Alfred A Knopf, Inc., 1994.

Nordstrom, Byron J., ed. *Dictionary of Scandinavian History*. Westport, CT: Greenwood Press, 1986.

BIBLIOGRAPHY

Blecher, George, and Lone Tygesen, eds. *Swedish Folk Tales and Legends*. New York: Pantheon Books, 1993.

Bruce-Jones, Stina, and Peter Graves. *Swedish Phrase Book*. London, England: Hugo's Language Books Unlimited, 1989.

CIA Factbook 2001 (http://www.odci.gov/cia).

Cornwallis, Graeme. *Lonely Planet: Sweden*. Oakland, CA: Lonely Planet Publications, 2000.

Countries of the World and Their Leaders, Yearbook 2002, vol. 2, pp. 1,213–1,217 Gale Group, Inc., 2001.

Culturenet Sweden. "Culturenet Sweden." 2002. Retrieved April 29, 2002 (http://www.kultur.nu/index.asp? language=1).

Daun, Åke. *Swedish Mentality*. Trans. Jan Teeland. University Park, PA: The Pennsylvania State University Press, 1996.

Davidson, H.R. Ellis. *Gods and Myths of Northern Europe*. New York: Penguin Books, 1964.

Föreningen Sverigeturism. "The Swedish Information Smorgasbord." 2002. Retrieved April 29, 2002 (http://www.sverigeturism.se/ smorgasbord/index.html).

Hård af Segerstad, Ulf. *Scandinavian Design*. New York: Lyle Stuart, 1961.

Icehotel. "Icehotel." 2002. Retrieved April 29, 2002 (http://www.icehotel.com).

Lahelma, Antti, and Johan Olofsson. "The Nordic FAQ." Lysator Academic Computer Society. 2001. Retrieved April 29, 2002 (http://www.lysator.liu.se/nordic/).

Lonely Planet: Sweden, 2000 (general country info).

Lorenzen, Lily. *Of Swedish Ways*. New York: Barnes and Noble Books, 1964.

Nordstrom, Byron J. *Scandinavia Since 1500*. Minneapolis, MN: The University of Minnesota Press, 2000.

Scobbie, Irene. *Sweden*. New York: Praeger Publishers, 1972.

Svenska Institutet. "The Swedish Institute." 2002. Retrieved April 29, 2002 (http://www.si.se/).

Svensson, Charlotte Rosen. *Culture Shock!: Sweden*. Portland, OR: Graphic Arts Center Publishing Company, 2000.

The Vasa Museum. "The Vasa Museum." 2002. Retrieved April 29, 2002 (http://www.vasamuseet.se/indexeng.html).

"Skolverket: The National Agency for Education." ed. Von Dewall, Gustaf. 2001. Retrieved April 29, 2002 (http://www.skolverket.se/english/ index.shtml).

Statistics Sweden. Retrieved April 29, 2002 (http://www.scb.se).

Waddams, Herbert. *The Swedish Church*. Westport, CT: Greenwood Press Publishers, 1981.

Worldmark Encyclopedia of the Nations, Europe, 8th ed, pp. 415–427. Public Gale Research Inc, 1995.

PRIMARY SOURCE IMAGE LIST

Page 22: This portrait of Gustav I dates circa 1550.

Page 23: This cave painting, discovered in Tanum, Bohuslan, Sweden, was created by the Boat-Axe people during the Bronze Age.

Page 24: This ninth-century stone carving, discovered in Gotland Island, Sweden, shows Viking navigation ritual and is currently housed at Statens Historiska Museet in Stockholm, Sweden.

Page 26 (top): Sweden's constitution of 1809 established a constitutional monarchy for the country.

Page 26 (bottom): This seventeenth-century Dutch line engraving depicts the Peace at Münster in May 1648, following the Thirty Years' War.

Page 27 (top): This eighteenth-century line engraving depicts the Russian fleet defeating the Swedish fleet at Cape Hango in July 1714.

Page 27 (bottom): This portrait of Peter the Great dates 1764 and is housed at the Blickling Property in Norfolk, Great Britain.

Page 28: Housed in the Swedish Emigrant Institute in Växjö, Sweden, this original poster encouraged Swedes to work as miners in California.

Page 28: This historical photograph housed at the Swedish Emigrant Institute in Växjö, Sweden, shows a crowd of people around the boat *Excelsior*, which brought Swedish immigrants to America.

Page 29: A cartoon titled "The Kindly Helping Hand" by Arthur Sjögren appeared in *Karbasesn* in 1901 and advocates suffrage for all men.

Page 30: This photograph of Sweden's parliament was taken at its opening ceremonies in 1939, which was at the start of Sweden's policy of neutrality.

Page 37: This painting titled *Crime* dates circa 1450 and is part of the National Law Codes of Magnus Eriksson, which is housed in the Uppsala University Collection, Sweden/Bridgeman Art Library.

Page 40: This twelfth-century Viking tapestry, which depicts the Viking gods Odin, Thor, and Freyr, is housed at the Statens Historiska Museet in Stockholm, Sweden.

Page 41: This Viking bronze amulet, located at the Statens Historiska Museet in Stockholm, Sweden, dates from the ninth century and represents a priest of the cult of Odin.

Page 42: This illustration from Finn Magnusen's *Eddalaeren* dates 1824 and represents Yggdrassil from Viking mythology.

Page 43: The Andreas Stone with a relief of a scene from the Norse poem Ragnarok, "Doomsday of the Gods," depicts the god Odin being eaten by the wolf Fenris. This stone relief, dating 1000, was discovered on the Isle of Man in England and is now located at the Manx Museum in the Isle of Man, England.

Page 44: This illustration from a seventeenth-century German text describes the witch trials in Sweden.

Page 46: This stone carving of the Viking god Loki from the late Viking period is housed at the Aarhus Museum of Art in Aarhus, Denmark.

Page 46: This illustration of witches during Midsummer's Night in Sweden appeared in the June 23, 1918, issue of *Allers Familj-Journal*.

Page 47: This illustration by John Bauer accompanied the fairy tale *The Sorceress and the Royal Children*.

Page 54: Alfred Nobel's laboratory, built in 1895, is part of the Nobel Museum in Karlskoga.

Page 54: This photograph was taken December 10, 2000, at the commencement of the Nobel Prize ceremony.

Page 55: Alfred Nobel signed his last will and testament on November 27, 1895, at the Swedish-Norwegian Club in Paris, France.

Page 57: This pendant of the goddess Freya from the Viking period in Sweden is housed at the Statens Historiska Museet in Stockholm, Sweden.

Page 58: Olaus Magnus created this illustration of victims burning in ancient Scandinavia in 1555 for his book *Historia gentibus septentrionalibus*.

Page 59: The Hammer of Thor, a Viking Talisman, was discovered in Ostergotland, Sweden, and dates from the tenth century AD.

Page 60: The Gannarve Stoneship is located in Gotland, Sweden, and dates from the Viking period.

Page 61: This illustration of German bishop Ansgar is from the book *Overland, Norges Historie* by an unknown author.

Page 61: This carving depicting a beheading dates 1160 and was found inside the tomb of Swedish King Eric IX, also known as Eric the Saint.

Page 62: This oil painting was completed during the late fifteenth century and portrays Christ appearing to Saint Bridget.

Page 66: This original oil painting by Anders Leonhard Zorn dates 1897 and shows Swedes dancing on Midsummer's Eve.

Page 71: The photograph of Stockholm's city library, Stadsbiblioteket, which was designed by Gunnar Asplund, was taken circa 1930.

Page 74: A watercolor painting by Carl Larsson titled *In the Hawthorn Hedge*.

Page 74: This sculpture by Carl Milles is displayed at the Carl Milles Museum in Stockholm, Sweden.

Page 75: This photograph of Anders Leonhard Zorn dates circa 1900.

Page 78: This studio portrait of Greta Garbo was taken circa 1935.

Page 78: A studio portrait of Ingrid Berman as Joan Madou in the 1948 film *Arch of Triumph*.

Page 80: A portrait of Swedish mystic and scientist Emanuel Swedenborg.

Page 81: Carolus Linnaeus's *Systema Naturae* was printed in Leyden in 1735.

Page 82: This portrait of Carl Michael Bellman is housed at the Royal Library in Stockholm.

Page 82: An unknown artist painted this portrait of Carolus Linnaeus circa 1760.

Page 83: This portrait of Swedish novelist and dramatist August Strindberg dates circa 1895.

Page 85: The original cover of Astrid Lindgren's *Pippi Longstocking*, a story that she created for her daughter in 1944.

Page 89: This advertisement for a concert given by Swedish singer Jenny Lind is housed at the Royal Library in Stockholm, Sweden.

Page 89: This photograph of the Swedish musical group ABBA was taken at a concert in 1979.

Page 108: This black-and-white steel engraving shows the Swedish-American inventor John Ericsson, who is responsible for establishing the principles of solar energy and inventing the ship propeller.

Page 108: This statue of a miner, which is located outside of the Falun copper mine in Sweden, was sculpted by Helge Zandén and erected in 1988.

Page 110: This photograph was taken as the first Volvo, Jakob, rolled out of the factory in 1927.

Page 110: Cover of the 2003 IKEA catalog.

Page 111: A Swedish advertisement for the match company Solstickan, which produces safety matches, an invention by chemistry professor Gustaf Erik Pasch in 1844. Swedish artist Einar Nerman designed the Solstickan Boy for these matchbooks.

INDEX

Sweden: A Primary Source Cultural Guide

About the Author

Jason Porterfield, a graduate of Oberlin College, lives in Chicago, Illinois.

Designer: Geri Giordano; **Cover Designer:** Tahara Hasan; **Editor:** Jill Jarnow;
Photo Researcher: Gillian Harper